From Neighborhood to Manhood

FROM
NEIGHBORHOOD
TO
MANHOOD

by

The Boys of Blue Hill Avenue

Edited by Arthur Bloom

Small Batch Books
Amherst, Massachusetts

SMALL
BATCH
BOOKS

493 South Pleasant Street
Amherst, Massachusetts 01002
413.230.3943
SMALLBATCHBOOKS.COM

IN MEMORIAM

Arthur Cohen
Michael Garber
Irving Zola

CONTENTS

Our Dorchester and Roxbury of the 1940s and 1950s

by
Arthur Bloom

THE WRITERS OF THE autobiographical essays that here follow grew up in the Boston neighborhoods of Dorchester
and Roxbury, which ranged from Blue Hill Avenue in Mattapan on one end to Grove Hall and Franklin Park on the other,
with the clear center of existence between Morton Street, at
Cutler's Pool Hall, and the G and G Delicatessen, several
blocks away. We went to Hebrew Schools in the area; were Bar
Mitzvahed in its synagogues; ate our first corned beef sandwiches and half-sour pickles at the G and G, where we would
sit talking for hours whiling away the breaks in our education;
hung out in our best suits at "The Wall" of Franklin Field during High Holy Days, looking for our female counterparts; and
later moved our activities over to the nearby Hecht House, as
we progressed through high school and approached college.

All this while our fathers worked to make a living, sometimes
but rarely with financial help from our mothers, whose role it
was in life more commonly to keep the kosher household and
prepare for Shabbat and the High Holidays, while raising us as
proper Jewish children. Life in that Dorchester and Roxbury

was not easy, but it had the inestimable virtue of bringing us close together in our families—though not always—and to our friends outside the family. The struggle just to get by financially, emotionally, was difficult for many of us and especially for our parents, but out of that struggle came a set of values that honed our survival skills and made us strong for our lives to come.

The Jewish community of Boston was, for most of the twentieth century, the fifth-largest Jewish community in the United States, with about 150,000 Jews; fewer earlier in the century and somewhat more as the century wore on. The community we came from had generated many distinguished leaders in American life, men like Supreme Court Justice Louis D. Brandeis, distinguished scientists like Professor Norbert Weiner of M.I.T., nationally esteemed rabbis like Israel Kazis of Temple Mishkan Tefila and Roland Gittelsohn of Temple Israel, and eminent physician-scientists like A. Clifford Barger, the physiologist of the Harvard Medical School, to name but a few.

Jews had been in Boston since Revolutionary times and before. Most of the early Jewish arrivals in the sixteenth and seventeenth centuries were Sephardic traders attached to English, Dutch or Italian trading companies. These traders did not, however, build permanent Jewish settlements in or around Boston, as the Massachusetts Bay Colony was first and foremost a religious haven for Puritans who did not welcome religious diversity—unlike, it should be added, the communities of traders in New York, Virginia and elsewhere. It is interesting, however, to note that proficiency in Hebrew had been made an entrance requirement at Harvard from its founding in 1636, reflecting the influence of the Old Testament, if not of the Jews, on Puritan Boston.

The growth of the Jewish community of Boston began in a serious but limited way in the mid-nineteenth century and was the result mainly of German and Polish immigration. These Jews, numbering about 3,000, at their peak settled in the South End of Boston, the South End being defined at that time as the area due south of the Boston Common. From there these German and Polish Jews moved to the suburbs of Roxbury and Brookline. Later in the nineteenth century, waves of Central and Eastern European Jewish immigrants arrived in Boston, settled primarily in enclaves in the North End, and were separate from the earlier immigrants socially, economically and in terms of their affiliations with specific synagogues.

By the end of the nineteenth century the North End was comprised of a mix of Jews, Italians and Irish, a seriously heterogeneous group, who lived in what might be called, on its face, a melting pot, but which in fact was more nearly an area of well-demarcated Jewish, Irish and Italian streets and neighborhoods. Statistically, there were, by 1895, approximately 7,700 Italians living in Boston's North End, alongside some 6,200 Jews. While the Italian population was to continue to grow in the North End in the early twentieth century—to 18,000 by 1905—the Jewish population of the North End fell to 4,700, as a result of outward migration of Jews to areas outside of downtown Boston.

By 1910, the Greater Boston Jewish population had risen to 100,000. Although Chelsea and Malden, towns to the north of Boston, absorbed many thousands of Jews, the real suburban focus of Boston Jewry became Roxbury and Dorchester, with, again, the Eastern European Jews making up the core of this migration. These "suburbs" were regarded as very desirable, with luxuriant Franklin Park at its core, along with comfortable homes and apartments and ready access by trolley to Boston proper. Thus the growth and development of Dorchester and Roxbury were initially a reflection of the commercial and professional success of Boston Jewry.

This success led to the building of synagogues—mostly

Conservative as time went on, but originally Orthodox in the Eastern European vein—which served as the focus of Jewish life in all the major areas of Roxbury and Dorchester, where the future members of Haym Salomon Aleph Tzadek Aleph (AZA) were born. This included the area in and around Blue Hill Avenue in Dorchester (site of the famous Blue Hill Avenue Synagogue), the extensions of Blue Hill Avenue to Grove Hall (home to Adath Jeshurun) and Elm Hill Avenue (where the Mishkan Tefila and the Crawford Street Synagogues were located), and then Mount Bowdoin and Mattapan. Ultimately, the population centers of Elm Hill and Grove Hall in Roxbury merged with the Franklin Park, Franklin Field and Mount Bowdoin sections of Dorchester and extended to the far reaches of Mattapan, which was an extension of Blue Hill Avenue. The Dorchester-Roxbury "suburbs" became, in time, the center of lower-middle-class and especially of working-class Jewish life of Boston, as wealthier Jews moved farther out from the city to Brookline, Newton and Waban.

Importantly for the boys of AZA, the Eastern and Central Europeans of late-nineteenth-century Boston established The Hebrew Industrial School, which became, under the guidance of Lina Hecht, a major center for the teaching of cooking, sewing and industrial arts—especially to Eastern European Jewish women. While Lina Hecht was the American-born wife of a German Jew, she was intent on also serving the boys and girls of the Eastern European Jewish Boston community, and so she moved her school to the West End from its origins in Boston's North End. Ultimately, in the twentieth century, the Hecht Neighborhood House relocated to the American Legion Highway in Dorchester, where it served as a community center, with meeting rooms, sports facilities and activities for all ages in the 1950s but especially for the young, prominent among them—the boys of Aleph Tzadek Aleph. (AZA was the name given to the group by its parent organization, B'nai B'rith, a charitable Jewish organization.)

It was at the Hecht House that our group of twenty-five to thirty, mainly Boston-area high school students met each Sunday afternoon to learn and follow Robert's Rules of Order, used in the democratic conduct of our weekly business. That business was oriented primarily to doing good works in the Jewish community, with our annual Scholarship Dance at the Totem Pole Dance Hall, which raised funds throughout the Dorchester and Roxbury community (and often beyond) for needy—and who wasn't?—Jewish college students. We did all manner of socially oriented works, but in so doing we fulfilled a serious emotional need of our adolescence: we became part of a group of bright, motivated young men—the girls had their own brand of B'nai B'rith—and we spent all our free time together, at one another's homes and at the Hecht House, doing socially acceptable things together, including partying.

The group members were mostly, though not only, students at the Boston Latin School. BLS—originally the Boys Latin School, founded in 1635 as a private preparatory school for Harvard—had a long and distinguished history of academic excellence, with rigorous training of young men in Latin, Greek, ancient history, etc. The masters at BLS were a proud and demanding lot, and that pride was instilled in the boys of Boston who were fortunate enough to be accepted for the seventh grade or the ninth grade, either by dint of their grades in elementary or junior high school or by dint of their performance on the Latin School entrance examinations. The Latin School was then a magnet for the "best and the brightest" in Boston, often coming from the working-class neighborhoods of Dorchester and Roxbury (the Jews) as well as South Boston and Jamaica Plain (the Irish) and East Boston and the North End (the Italians). In fact, in response to the rigors of the school and the relative social segregation, the Jews became more Jewish, and the Irish and Italians more Catholic, with an occasional

Protestant finding his way with difficulty among us.

Thus the young men of Aleph Tzadek Aleph, who assembled under the name of Haym Salomon, an early Jewish merchant of Revolutionary times, were a proud group, many of whom withstood together the slings and arrows of their Latin School masters and the dislike of their Irish Catholic harassers on the streets of Boston. They, we, studied together, played together, suffered together, all in the expectation that we would go on, somehow, from these modest beginnings to decent colleges—many expected to be and were accepted at Harvard, which took almost 100 Boston Latin School boys in 1952, the year of graduation from BLS for most of us—and to careers as lawyers, doctors, accountants, researchers, teachers, writers, whatever we (and our mothers) wanted us to be. We had dreams, and those dreams were often fulfilled, as the stories that follow here attest.

To have grown up in the Dorchester and Roxbury of those times was a privilege: I say this not because it was materially rich, for it was decidedly not, but because it was spiritually rich. In the Jewish community, or at least in our segment of that Jewish community, we all cared for one another, looked out for one another. There was an emotional bond that united us; we had our own unique culture and context. And, of course, in no small measure the birth in 1948 of the State of Israel generated in those of us who were teenagers at the time a pride which was a fierce antidote to the anger we felt at the extermination of European Jews—our kin, after all—by the Nazis.

I would argue that the lives described in the following pages represent at least partial fulfillment of the ideals of the American immigrant experience. We of Haym Salomon AZA were luckier than many: we had our own cohesive social group in adolescence and beyond; we had the support generally of our families, for whom our success was very important per se and as a measure of their own achievements in this land in which they were either first- or second-generation immigrants; plus we were well educated and had the opportunity to succeed. Through it all, our affection, nay love, for one another was sustaining, and we have in recent years rediscovered that love and, mirabile dictu, it is intact as we now proceed into our mid-seventies.

We are pleased to share these stories of our lives with you: our children, our friends, and our readers more broadly interested in the history of a group of young men from Boston who went on to lead lives of achievement and satisfaction, while never forgetting whence they came.

Reference: *The Jews of Boston*, J.D. Sarna, E. Smith, S-M. Kosofsky (eds.), Yale University Press, New Haven and London, in assoc. with The Combined Jewish Philanthropies of Greater Boston, 2005. See especially: "The Jews of Boston in Historical Perspective," by J.D. Sarna, pp. 3-18; "From Margin to Mainstream," by L.A. Jick, pp.87-104; and "In Search of Suburbs: Boston's Jewish Districts, 1843-1994," G.H.Gamm, pp. 137-173.

CHAPTER ONE

Sumner (Zummie) Katz

IT IS MAY, 2008. I will soon be off to Boston from the Washington, D.C., area, where I live, to attend the funeral of an aunt, one of eight children on my mother's side who was born in Chelsea, Massachusetts, just outside of Boston. Two of the eight were male, but one died as a child in a street accident. My mother was the oldest, born in 1908, one year after my grandmother came to America to join my grandfather. He had been here five years already, having joined family who crossed the ocean from Russia and Poland even earlier. Family members helped one another, first to travel, then to survive, and then to thrive. My maternal grandfather's family name was Ribock. My grandmother's family name was Schweiloch, which mysteriously became Sevinor in this country. I was part of what had become a huge extended family. It numbered in the hundreds when it convened to celebrate Purim each year in a hall in Chelsea when I was a kid.

My mother, as I said, was born in this country. Being the eldest in a large family, she became at an early age a second mother to her siblings. From what I've been told, that left little room and time for her to have a childhood of her own.

Another development as a child affected her life deeply and forever. She contracted polio at the age of nine or ten. The polio ravaged the muscles in her legs, especially her right one, and even after several operations to extend the contracted muscles, she was left with one leg significantly shorter than the other. This had an impact on her walking and on her balance. She could no longer run. But one (of many) amazing things about her: she never asked any quarter about her disability, not as a teenager helping her mother at home as well as her father in his business, not as a wife and mother running a busy and demanding household, and not as a senior, when she eventually grudgingly relented and began to use a cane and a walker very late in life. She lived to ninety-eight.

I am the second of four brothers. By her third child, my mother was desperate to have a girl. It was not to be. One of my aunts had four girls and was equally interested in having a boy. I have recently been told, but I can't vouch for its accuracy, that related families facing similar desires and disappointments in the "old country" might well have arranged a swap of one of the boys for one of the girls. This was especially important for the family that lacked a male heir. Not in this country, of course. So my mother was stuck with all four of us.

Like my mother, I was born in Chelsea, and I spent my first six years there. Chelsea is a small, independent city just north across the Mystic River from Boston. It had a large immigrant-based Jewish population then, and we were part of it. We lived in an apartment directly across from my grandparents' home.

My father came to this country in 1924 from Lithuania. He was sixteen at the time. His travel was arranged and financed by his family. His mother had died when he was young, and his father, a fisherman by trade, had remarried. My father was unhappy, and though a good student already studying at a yeshiva in Vilna, jumped at the opportunity to go to America. He spent several years in New York with family, delivering meat, learning English, etc. He later moved to Chelsea, where there was additional family, and began working in my grandfather Ribock's coal yard. He met my mother, who also was working there. They eventually married and had their first son in 1931.

An uncle, Isaac (Tim) Tarmy, later also worked in my grandfather's coal yard. Uncle Tim, as a freshman at MIT, had eloped with my aunt "Honey" (Helen). This was the end of MIT for him, since, as a husband, he had to start earning a living. My father and uncle encouraged my grandfather to add lumber to his articles for sale, and he finally relented. Disputes, however, continued among them. Finally, my father (William, nicknamed "Wolfie") and Uncle Tim borrowed several thousand dollars from Tim's father to begin a lumber business. They rented a long shed and some property with railroad siding from the railroad that owned a huge depot only several blocks from Copley Square and the Boston Public Library. That was in 1937. They rented the property for twenty years, until they were evicted and had to move the lumberyard to another location. They were forced to make way for the beginning of Boston's modern transformation, the development of the Prudential Center and related commercial enterprises at that same location, the former rail depot.

When I was six, in 1940, we moved from Chelsea to Dorchester, an enclave of Boston, into a two-family house. Who moved above us? Family, of course: my Uncle Tim and Aunt Honey, and their children. Within a couple of years, another aunt and uncle (Zelda and Louis) and their children moved into a two-family home only two houses away. I will always remember my first day of school in Dorchester. It was December. I was in the first grade, and I was terrified. Not a familiar face except my mother's, and when she left, the tears really flowed.

Eventually I got my bearings. I was fortunate to be a good student, always conscientious, always anxious, and always disappointed if my test papers were not those selected to be shown on the walls. Though short in stature, I was blessed with speed and strength for the many street and field games that were then current. My days and weeks were busy, since I had to attend not only elementary school, but Hebrew school as well. Four days a week, I would walk about a mile after public school to learn Hebrew and related topics for two more hours. Then walk back. This would be repeated on Sunday mornings, unless I got a lift from my father. On Saturdays, friends and I would walk a similar distance to play baseball or football at the local field. And on a Saturday afternoon you could usually catch me at the Morton Theatre, a local movie house, which usually presented two features, a news round-up, and serial cartoons.

Boston and its subdivisions were clearly delineated by ethnic and religious groups. Dorchester and its neighboring Roxbury and Mattapan were no different. Not surprisingly, we lived in the Jewish area. Among others there were Irish, Italian, and Black sections as well. My long street was, in fact, divided: the first third Jewish and the remainder Irish.

We did not have to be told more than once not to wander into "hostile" territory, especially alone. By and large if you stayed in your own section, you had little to worry about. But incidents would occur. One winter day while walking home with my younger brother Burt from an afternoon at the movies, two Irish kids making anti-Semitic remarks approached us. They were both bigger than I. Thinking quickly, I said that two against one (Burt was too young to count then) was unfair and urged them to wrestle me one at a time. I was lucky and strong enough to wrestle each of them to the ground, and Burt and I continued safely home.

Sunday afternoons, we frequently visited family. Most often we traveled upwards of forty-five minutes from Dorchester back to Chelsea to visit grandparents and the many family members still in that area. We had to drive through the Sumner Tunnel in downtown Boston to get to Chelsea. Since my name was Sumner (although to this day family and old friends call me "Zummie," a derivative of my Hebrew name "Zalman"), I would inevitably yell throughout the length of the tunnel that it was "my tunnel."

And so the days and years of my early youth flowed by, filled with family, school, many neighborhood friends, sports, and street games.

By age thirteen many things had changed. I became a Bar Mitzvah in December, 1947. Several months earlier, my grandfather on my father's side joined our household. He survived the Holocaust, as did my Uncle Norman, who was able to leave a deportation camp with his wife and other relatives to come to this country a few years later. Norman has written an account of those mad years describing how, when a late teenager, he had fled from a firing squad into nearby woods, how he had eventually linked up with my grandfather, and how they had survived three years by working for a farmer and hiding in barns and underground to evade Nazi patrols and local vigilantes. A frightening and stunning story—one that I was not told about until recent years because no one at that time wanted to or could talk about those horrendous times. In addition, we children were understandably protected from hearing about such horrid events. Two aunts, my father's sisters, had fortunately left Eastern Europe for Palestine in the late 1930s. They were dedicated Zionists and socialists. They helped establish a kibbutz in northern Israel, fought the British after World War II and invading Arabs thereafter, and raised families. I would finally meet them in 1956 on my first trip to Israel.

My father's and uncle's lumber business, General Builders Supply Co., survived the war—like others, it was allotted a fair share of supplies and material during that period. After the war, the business really thrived as part of the pent-up residential and commercial building boom. As my brothers and I reached our teens, we were expected to work in the yard during summers.

Any resistance to such work was counteracted forcefully by my mother. We would wait on customers, load up trucks for deliveries, unload rail cars filled to the brim with lumber from the West Coast or the South, and when older actually make deliveries. Eventually, three brothers went into the business. I decided against it, which I'll discuss in more detail later. After my father passed in 1969, at the young age of sixty-one, there was what can only be described as a typical family feud over who would run and own the business. It was eventually divided up among those who were interested, with my older brother Herb, for various reasons, ending up with its core. My youngest brother, Len, to this day runs his own lumberyard in Cambridge, Massachussets, and brother Burt is in the construction business in the Detroit area.

Herb is four years older than I. Burt is four years younger, and Len is yet another four years younger than Burt. Herb led the way in many respects, and I for some time followed in his footsteps, hoping of course to do even better.

For example, by age thirteen I had followed Herb into the Boston Public Latin School, the one public school in Boston that rigorously prepared you for acceptance into the best colleges in the country, most especially Harvard. At that time it was an all-boys school, with a much smaller separate sister school across the street. To enter this school in the seventh grade, one had to have excellent grades in elementary school, or pass a qualification test. I've always studied hard, and with some success as I mentioned earlier, and I was accepted on the basis of my grades. Perhaps two hundred more boys were later admitted in the ninth grade. All told, over 700 students were admitted to my 1952 graduation class in either the seventh or ninth grade, but less than 200 actually graduated. I recall spending, from the seventh grade on, no less than two to three hours a day on homework, frequently more.

Going to Latin School was a divide of a sort for me. Of

the tens of kids I went to school with and played with in the neighborhood, only two or three went to Latin. The rest moved on to local junior high schools, and later yet to one of several available high schools spread around the city. My life and daily routine really diverged from theirs. Old friendships weakened and new ones arose, including with many of those represented in this book.

Boston Latin, as it turned out, was only a few minutes from my dad's lumberyard near downtown Boston. As a result, my dad was able to drive me and several others to Latin School daily. To get home, I had to take a street car, then the subway and then a bus, rides totaling close to an hour.

As mentioned above, going to Boston Latin led to a host of major changes in my daily life. "Real life," if you will, began to impinge, in that success there—we were led to understand—led to a college of one's choice and eventually to an esteemed career in some profession. Being forced to drop out, as so many of my classmates were, would be almost tantamount to failing in life. Or so I was led to believe.

I don't recall even considering not going to Latin School. My brother Herb had already survived four years there when it was my time to decide. His grades were good, he was a good athlete, and two years after I matriculated, he was accepted into Harvard and Dartmouth, choosing Dartmouth. I could do no less, I thought.

Another development in my early teens was my folk's acquisition of an old, large beach house on "K" street in Nantasket (or Hull). It was only a few houses from the beach, as was the succeeding house we lived in on "J" Street. Each year, right after school's end, the family (most of all, my mother) would pack what we needed. We would then load up one of my father's lumber trucks and head for the beach for the summer. Nantasket is south of Boston in the direction of Cape Cod, only a forty-five-minute ride at that time to downtown Boston. My father commuted each day, and I did so with him beginning in my late teens when I worked in the lumberyard.

My summers at Nantasket are among my fondest memories. I loved the waves and the water, cold as it was through much of the summer. I loved playing baseball for several years for the town team. The whole team would tumble into the coach's car to travel to a neighboring town for a game. After many of those games, the coach would take us to nearby quarries for diving and swimming in our birthday suits. I loved when friends could visit for the weekends. They would sleep in an unfinished attic strewn with mattresses, and my mother would make sure they didn't go hungry. My friends and I would enjoy all the beach had to offer: the water and ball games, of course, but also, in our later teens, the lovely blossoming girls. Crowds of teenagers would gather in a section called Kenberma, and we would think nothing of walking a mile to get there and ogle. On rainy days, I loved going to the local movie house, a converted yellow barn only two streets from my house. I loved the fact that once again, we were surrounded by family and friends who bought places as close as next door and no further than a few blocks away. I loved going fishing for the day with my father, uncle, and family friends. It was one of the few activities of the sort that I did with my father. He was relaxed, and my Uncle Tim and family friend Abe Carver were wonderful in recalling and telling jokes. Laughter reigned and the fish went generally unscathed. When we did catch a few, my father, given his own childhood experiences in Eastern Europe, cleaned them. It was the only household activity I ever saw my father engage in. No, I take that back, he did make hamburgers and hot dogs on the outdoor grill while my mother did everything else in the kitchen. That was her domain. She rarely asked any of us, her husband or her four sons, to help in the kitchen—or anywhere else in the house, for that matter.

I am looking now at the write-up of myself in the Boston

Latin School graduation book for 1952. My nickname "Zummie" is there followed by the aphorism (there was one for each of those graduating) "Great oaks from little acorns grow." I was still a "little acorn," not having grown much through those years. Nor did I become a "great oak" in later years. I did, though—I suppose—shine somewhat there. I played baseball and football and ran track. I was awarded a number of academic prizes and was selected for the National Honor Society. In my senior year, I was elected president of the society and, as such, gave a speech at the graduation ceremony. My election as president was, if I recall correctly, by the narrowest of margins. I thought for a time that I was running unopposed and did little to harness votes, only to be informed by close friends several days before the election that a classmate, Bob Gargill, was quite successfully soliciting votes. My friends urged me to do the same and fortunately I heeded their advice and won. Bob went on to have an eminent legal career in Boston and I, as will be explained in a little more detail, went on to Washington, D.C., where I had, in effect, three different careers.

The graduation book also indicated that I was a member of a number of clubs (German Club, Camera Club, Literary Club, etc.), and that I was "1st Lt., 1st Co, 2nd Regt." Both the clubs and the military rank deserve a few words. As for the clubs, Lee Dunn, the school's college placement counselor, urged all students to join as many clubs and activities as possible, the aim being to include them in college applications and impress college admissions officers. Mr. Dunn had an incredible track record and a very special relationship with the admissions office at Harvard. The result? Over 100, in excess of fifty percent of our graduation class, were admitted to Harvard. Not all decided to go there, which included myself. (Several years later, Mr. Dunn retired and the admission figures at Harvard dropped dramatically).

As for my military rank, all students were required to

participate in ROTC (Reserve Officer Training Corps). As they rose from the seventh grade (called Class VI at Latin School) to their senior year (Class I) one might receive promotions and end up with a lofty rank such as captain or first lieutenant We had khaki uniforms, weekly drill classes, and periodic "military reviews." There was an annual city parade, consisting of bands and regiments from all the Boston high schools. Those schools performing best won awards. Latin School had many such awards proudly displayed in its halls.

These teen years were busy, then, with school, homework, school sports, and other activities. They were, at least for me, somewhat serious because the "track" I was on at Latin School required daily dedication and my best efforts. School also brought me in touch with a whole new group of boys, boys not from my immediate neighborhood and elementary school. Many of these boys and I in our mid-teens joined the Haym Salomon AZA It was a Jewish youth group sponsored by the local chapter of B'nai B'rith, a men's group.

My father and uncle were active in B'nai B'rith, and my Uncle Tim was an official advisor to the youth group. Both were also prominent in the local community. My father, for example, became president of a temple in Dorchester and a board member of a local bank. Later, after leaving Dorchester for the suburbs, he again became president of a local temple and he was active on boards of Jewish educational institutions in the Boston area.

Returning to the subject of the AZA, that youth group cemented friendships already begun in school and added yet more friends. It was an active organization. We had monthly meetings—sometimes in my house; we had sports teams; we had socials with corresponding girls' groups; and we participated in regional youth group activities. Our main event was an annual live-band dance in a large dance hall in Newton. The net proceeds from the dance funded college scholarships, so our aim was to attract as many teenagers from the Boston area to the dance as possible, and to do the same for business ads in our dance program. For months the entire chapter worked on the dance. With at least several hundred attending each year, the dance was usually a smashing success and we all reveled in it. One thing I recall doing for it each year was to garner a number of business ads for the program. Some were from local Dorchester neighborhood businesses, but others were the result of a trip I took each year back to Chelsea, my birthplace. There, beginning with my grandfather's still-active cement business and lumberyard, I would walk up and down the streets of the city's industrial and commercial area, introduce myself as my grandfather's kin, and solicit ads. There was an occasional refusal, but not many.

My best friends were in the AZA group. We laughed together a lot; we studied and worried together a lot; we went to socials together, double- or triple-dated together, went to the beach and skiing together, etc. It was supportive. I felt valued. I felt fortunate, but at the same time there was a twinge of guilt because many of these friends were growing up in households more modest than my own.

Most of them were headed to Harvard from Boston Latin School, some with scholarships, many beginning their college careers by commuting from their homes in Dorchester or nearby Roxbury and Mattapan to Cambridge. Financially, it was their only option. By the time I was a senior in high school, I was off on a different track. I'm not sure when it began, but I felt the need to break away from the security blanket I have been trying to describe. I felt the need to do something first rather than simply follow in familiar and expected footsteps. So rather than go to Harvard with my friends, or to Dartmouth, where my brother had just graduated, I decided to go someplace where I knew no one, where no one knew me, and where, I thought, I would have the opportunity and freedom to make my own way. Being lucky enough to have a choice, I chose Yale. To someone who had been out of the Boston area for only a weekend in New York City with my father, and for three summer camps in Maine and Massachusetts, New Haven felt as if it were my brave new world. In retrospect I probably bit off more than I could chew.

Perhaps that last sentence is somewhat of an exaggeration. More probably, I would have had a mixed college experience wherever I went. I say "mixed" because academically I continued to do well, graduating magna cum laude, but it was an emotionally fraught and somewhat directionless experience. "Directionless" because I could not, for the life of me, decide what profession or line of work to pursue. I seemed to perform equally well in whatever courses I took. I did not seem to be interested enough in the sciences to focus on them, and there was such a vast array of other courses! I thought I liked history. I thought I liked political science. I thought I liked sociology and psychology. But none of them enough to major in. It was a continuous problem throughout my four years at Yale.

I made some good friends at Yale and cherish them to this day. I wandered all over the lot intellectually, including wandering away from Jewish roots and ties. Dating was not simple, for many of the girls' colleges (Smith, Vassar, UConn) were hours away by car. Traveling two to three hours for a Saturday night date that ended at midnight, and then returning to New Haven, was not easy, and there was the occasional serious accident. So if you were lucky, you met a compatible girl in or around New Haven. I was, and I recall dating one in my sophomore year and another in my senior year fairly seriously. The relationship in my senior year was heading toward possible matrimony and I backed away in much confusion and guilt.

I was not a joiner in college. I did not join a fraternity. Nor was I invited to join the George Bush's Skull and Bones or any similar exclusive shop. I did not embrace Hillel, the Jewish student organization, because I was stumbling over my identity. After a freshman stint at the Wright dormitory in the Yale Yard, I and three new friends roomed together for the next three years at Jonathan Edwards residential college. Each "college" (there were nine or ten then) had a live-in master, who was also a member of the faculty, and a number of other professors specifically associated with the college. Those faculty offered seminars, special studies, and counseling services to residents. The format worked well. It helped break down a large university into meaningful, supportive smaller pieces. These colleges also sponsored a number of musical, theatrical and social events. High on Jonathan Edwards's list were the annual production of a Gilbert and Sullivan play (in which my roommate Al Atkins always played a major role) and the annual toga party (which, fortunately or unfortunately, had major limits concerning alcohol use and other activities that were consistent with the times).

So I studied a lot at Yale. I worried a lot. I struggled, to no avail, to give myself a sense of direction. I drank coffee and smoked much too much in the local Bickford's cafeteria while trying to write a paper or study for an exam. If I had to select one image of myself at Yale, it would be that one in the cafeteria.

Senior year came soon enough. Some kind of decision had to be made about where to go from there. I suppose I could have gone into my father's business, but that also was not attractive. I ended up, without much investigation or knowledge, applying to several law schools. I was again fortunate enough to have a choice and this time I chose Harvard.

Going to Harvard Law School brought me home again, among family and some old friends still in the Boston area. But it did not bring me any nearer to a sense of direction or a goal that I wanted to pursue. Quite the contrary. Property, civil procedure, tort and other first-year law courses simply did not capture my interest or imagination. I was sorely disappointed and, for the first time in my life, I was unable to stay focused and study, not even for the sake of good grades, if for no other reason. I started by commuting from home to classes. Home by then was in Newton, a suburb of Boston. My folks had moved there from Dorchester shortly after I left for Yale. Many families, Jewish and other, were beginning to make the upwardly mobile trek from Dorchester and nearby communities of Boston proper to the suburbs. Years later, amid ethnic and racial conflicts, that trickle to the outskirts would turn into a surge.

Although home was physically in Newton, in my heart "home" remained in Dorchester. (My bothers Burt and Len, on the other hand, grew up in Newton and consider that "home.") Commuting to law school didn't work so I moved into Ames Hall, a dormitory on the school campus. One of my roommates from Yale, Dave Linett, already lived there. That was helpful, but not helpful enough to change my attitudes or grade level. Second-year law courses were equally disappointing to me (corporations, taxation, etc). But the second year brought a major distraction as well. Early in the school year I met, totally by accident, an old friend, Irving Zola, in an Italian restaurant in East Boston. He was with a young woman, who was soon to become his first wife, and that woman's new roommate at Boston University graduate school was, within a year and a half, to become my first wife. Our relationship was, from the beginning, tumultuous and ended before the close of the school year, or so it seemed at the time. I had by then had enough of law school, but rather than quit I took a rare, but not unheard of year's leave-of-absence. During that year I got my military service "out of the way" with six months active duty at Fort Dix, New Jersey. While on weekend leaves from Fort Dix, I reconnected with my wife-to-be in New York City. Not too many months later we were married at a hastily arranged ceremony in a waiting room in a New York City hospital. No, she was not pregnant. It was just that living at home in Brooklyn had become intolerable for her, and her father was to be in a hospital for several weeks recuperating from a leg fracture suffered during a robbery at his office. Immediate family and some friends joined us. Needless to say, neither my folks nor hers were terribly happy about it all.

Once married, I had to think practically for a change. I decided to go back to Cambridge for my third year of law school and the L.L.B. degree. The third year was both more interesting (e.g., optional courses such as a seminar on the criminal justice system) and productive. I graduated with a prize, albeit one of mixed import, of being the most-improved third-year law student of the class.

With this less-than-happy legal studies experience, I sought other avenues of work after graduation. I found what I hoped to be a rewarding route, a federal-government-wide intern program. I was attracted by the idea of public service, of giving something back to society, of doing something "worthwhile." I was young and idealistic. I was not interested in making a lot of money. I was married and wanted to provide security and a certain level of comfort for us but not necessarily much more than that.

As expected, my folks were not pleased with my decision. Although my father was a liberal and a Democrat, as were most Jews following the victory over Hitler and Truman's support of the founding of the State of Israel, he did not share my view of government service. His well-educated son should, he not surprisingly hoped, pursue a legal or business career in Boston. The idea of my not doing so and living so far away in Washington, D.C., was very hard for me to explain and even harder for him to accept. My mother was equally disappointed, but less vocal on the subject.

There was vigorous competition to enter this intern program. There were written exams. There were arranged group discussions among the applicants, during which one's participation was assessed. I felt fortunate to be selected. It was then my responsibility to go to Washington and arrange interviews with agencies and departments that interested me. I had several interviews and was most intrigued with the international program and the people at the U.S. Information Agency. That agency, of which the better-known Voice of America was a part, also ran libraries overseas, helped implement the Fulbright Exchange Program, and engaged in a host of other activities. It was part of the country's extensive international affairs machinery during the height of the Cold War. Several years ago the agency was disbanded and its pieces spread ignominiously among the many tentacles of the Department of State.

Prior to beginning work in the summer of 1960 at the U.S. Information Agency, I took and passed the D.C. bar exam, the rewards of which became apparent only years later. I reported for work with five other young persons that summer. We were management interns. We trained for the better part of a year, rotating six weeks at a time among the various administrative divisions, such as budget and personnel, and among program-related offices as well, such as the European Affairs Division or the Publications Division.

My fellow interns were eager and bright. Agency management had decided several years earlier to recruit actively among prospective interns, believing that such an effort would pay off handsomely in the long run. They were right, for interns employed during those several years eventually rose to some of the highest ranks both at USIA and in other agencies. Many of them became friends, some lifelong. We were all new to Washington and to government.

After the year of internship, my first assignment was to the Program and Budget Division. This division was central to the agency, not only for its role in obtaining funds from Congress, but also for developing programs and projects and overseeing the implementation and control of the agency's budget. It was headed at that time by an extremely capable career employee,

Ben Posner. Ben was also a major proponent in the agency of bringing in these young interns I have been describing, and he already had a number of them placed in his division when I arrived.

I began work in the Near East and South Asia section of the division under the tutelage of a kind and pleasant gentleman named Carl Malmi. There was a lot of detail to be mastered about the agency's programs in the countries in those areas. Carl and I had to prepare budgets and explanatory material for the agency's annual budget request to Congress. We attended congressional hearings and helped the agency's leadership defend the request against the merciless questioning of Representative Rooney, a multi-decade congressman from Brooklyn, New York. We spent a lot of time on special projects. One of those concerned how to spend constructively the government's excess Indian rupees. They were excess in that the rupees the Indian government paid for agricultural products, under what then was called the P.L. 480 surplus agricultural program, had to be spent only in that country. Those rupees far exceeded the normal needs of our government in India.

In addition to working with Carl, I taught American history at a small junior college in Washington. In 1963 I was asked if I were interested in going to Monrovia, Liberia, to be an executive officer of the new Voice of America radio relay station in that country. The station was built to receive, enhance, and redirect radio signals broadcast originally from the Washington studios in a number of languages, including Russian, English, Hindi, Polish and Urdu. I was torn. I looked forward to an overseas assignment, but Liberia was far and unknown, my first child, Anita, was only six months old, and my family was sure to be shocked. After going back and forth on the prospect for several weeks, I finally decided to give it a try.

The only way to travel fairly quickly to Liberia in those days was to fly to Paris and from there to West Africa, on Air France.

Because Paris is such a pleasure to visit, we stayed for several days before moving on. I had been there in 1956, when I was traveling around Western Europe during the summer after graduating Yale. Two old high school friends, Irving Zola and Henry Heifetz, also planned to go, but had to cancel at the last minute for financial reasons. The trip to Europe was by ship. The ocean was rough, so my most poignant memory of it is leaning over the side of the ship alongside many others. In addition to touring some on the continent, I went to Israel for two weeks to visit my aunts and their families in Tel Aviv and in Kibbutz Dafne on the Lebanon border. The trip there was most memorable, not only for the opportunity to meet and stay with the families and observe how they lived, but also for my first visits to Jerusalem; to Eilath, at the edge of the desert at the tip of southern Israel; to the Sea of Galilee; and to so many other localities in the country.

To present in some detail the years spent in Liberia would be a chapter in and of itself. But briefly, as an executive officer of the radio relay station, my work involved a wide variety of functions, including liaison with the U.S. embassy, personnel and budget matters, supervision of a local staff of fifteen, etc. Our offices were in downtown Monrovia, across from the U.S. embassy. The relay station was about twenty-five miles away, just off the one asphalt road that ran out of Monrovia. The road was only fifty miles long, built just several years earlier with U.S. aid funds. It ran from downtown Monrovia through the huge Firestone rubber plantation, past the airport, and ended at President Tubman's mansion.

The President was a descendant of ex-American slaves who had been shipped to Liberia in the mid-nineteenth century as part of a scheme to try to resolve the slavery issue. By the 1960s he and about 20,000 other descendants controlled both the country and between one and one and a half million indigenous people. This non-inclusiveness was a major contributing factor to the coup and ensuing massacres by Charles Taylor in the 1980s and 1990s.

Our residence in Liberia was a two-bedroom bungalow, one of five rented by the Voice of America in that immediate area. Our accommodations were comfortable enough but the water had to be boiled, the iguanas on the walls had to be tolerated, and the equatorial heat had to be borne. There were frequent crises with our locally hired staff, one of which involved a walk-out of all security personnel hired by one of our contractors. Because of rampant theft, it was critical to induce the contractor and his employees to resolve their disputes as quickly as possible. That we did.

There was little to do in Monrovia itself. There was much entertainment in homes. There was also "upcountry" travel to isolated small villages. Those visits were facilitated by Peace Corps volunteers dispersed throughout the country. It was the largest Peace Corps program in the world at that time. Its focus was on education. Other travel involved trips to countries on the west coast of Africa, including the Ivory Coast, Ghana and Nigeria.

From Liberia we returned to the States and I resumed work in the agency's Program and Budget Division. In 1966, I was asked to participate in a new government-wide effort to improve its planning, programming and budgeting processes. The first step was education. Twelve eager, relatively young employees, all from different agencies, were sent to Stanford University for a year's study in systems analysis and operations research. Stanford was one of six or seven participating universities. I chose Stanford because it gave me a chance to see the West Coast for the first time, and much of the rest of the country as well on our trips to and from the coast. It was a wonderful year, not only for all the new sights and sounds, especially those in San Francisco, but also for the new friendships made among my fellow students and the intellectual challenges presented. My children,

Anita and Larry, were three and one, respectively. I remember so clearly Anita's checkered red and black coat in the cool, rainy weather, and Larry's first efforts to walk and then to climb the one step to the porch of our rented house in Mountain View, just south of Palo Alto.

Upon our return to Washington, my major task was to help develop an agency-wide planning and programming system that would assist top agency personnel to make decisions on the most effective uses of limited resources. It was a complex task. It took more than a year to develop and the better part of another year to educate employees worldwide in the use of the system. I was part of that education process, teaching fellow workers as close as next door, as far away as Australia, and in many countries in between—such as Morocco, India, Thailand, Laos and Singapore.

Always a bit restless and searching, I turned my eyes back to academia in 1969 and was accepted into the John Hopkins University's graduate program in political science. I had a little money saved, enough to get us through an academic year, so I thought I would give it a try. My wife at that time also began a long career teaching theatre at Howard University. Despite the long commute three to four days a week from Washington to Baltimore, I enjoyed the study, but not enough to pursue it further. The political science field was rapidly emphasizing the use of quantitative analysis techniques, which were neither my forte nor my interest. So the following year I returned to the U.S. Information Agency and, in my spare time, researched and wrote my master's thesis on the urban renewal program, more specifically on the impact that citizen participation and a systems planning approach could be expected to have on the program.

I then spent a couple of more years with the agency, this time in the Office of the Director working on special studies and projects. Those studies included an effort to develop priorities among the Voice of America's many language broadcasts and an inquiry into the future of the agency's extensive overseas library operations. When my interest in the agency began to wane I turned to assets that I had made no use of until then, my law degree and related membership in the District of Columbia Bar, and I embarked on what could be described as my second career. My degree was over ten years old, and I had never practiced law; but it did not take me too long to find a job as an attorney with the National Association of Regulatory Utility Commissioners (NARUC). NARUC is an association of state utility regulatory commissioners with responsibilities similar to many associations in Washington, i.e., lobbying, litigation and providing relevant information to its members on developments in the federal city. All utilities were under its purview: telecommunications, gas, electric, cable, railroads, interstate trucking, and airlines. The association was also involved in early programs aimed at energy conservation. Its main goal was to protect and enhance state authority against federal encroachment. My title was assistant general counsel. My responsibilities included drafting legislation, preparing testimony for congressional hearings, and preparing position papers and testimony on federal rules proposed by agencies such as the Federal Communications Commission (FCC), the Federal Power Commission (now FERC), the Interstate Commerce Commission (ICC), and the Civil Aeronautics Board (CAB). The association also ran huge annual conventions which took me to places such as Seattle and Atlanta for the first time.

Much of my time with the association involved participation in court proceedings, especially preparation of appellate briefs. One case, I recall, involved Southwest Airline's early efforts to expand its intrastate offerings in the Dallas–Fort Worth area. The federal government opposed the expansion, and we filed an amicus curiae brief in the federal appellate court in support of the state commission's and Southwest's position. Southwest eventually won.

In another matter, which went to the U.S. Supreme Court, an attorney for the National Association of Railroad Passengers and I both wrote briefs in support of a state law which had required railroads to adhere to several state safety requirements. We shared the oral argument before the Supreme Court and I, for one, was extremely nervous. The court was cordial, but eventfully rejected our positions on the grounds of federal preemption of state authority in this area of the law.

After several years with the association, I found in 1977 other utility-related work in the general counsel's office of the General Services Administration (GSA). Among a wide array of duties, that office was also responsible for representing the federal government in proceedings before both federal and state regulatory commissions involving utility matters. The field was immense and the lawyers few, so the office had to be quite selective in matters it became involved in. For example, providing telecommunications to federal agencies was a major responsibility of GSA, so we utility lawyers focused a lot on communication matters pending both before the FCC and Congress. The breakup of AT&T was taking place during my stay with the agency, and the developing legislation and the ensuing regulatory and court battles consumed much of my time for several years.

Another major responsibility I had there was to represent the government in utility rate-setting matters before state regulatory commissions. These cases could last several weeks and involved the usual panoply of trial-related work, such as preparing and putting witnesses on the stand, cross-examination of the utility's witnesses, preparing and defending motions, writing briefs, etc. The government in many jurisdictions was a major consumer and had an interest in keeping its expenses as low as possible. I litigated such cases in a number of jurisdictions, including Maryland, the District of Columbia, Missouri and New York. This litigation experience would be critical to my third career, which I'll discuss below. By early 1982, I was appointed chief counsel of the utility intervention program at GSA. In that position I also supervised the efforts of other attorneys. We continued to intervene in as many state utility rate cases as we could, and to represent the government's interest in both rate and rulemaking proceedings before federal regulatory agencies.

Those were busy years at GSA, but fraught as well. My first wife and I were experiencing more and more tension and separateness, which drove us apart by the late 1970s. Our two children, Larry and Anita, were sixteen and fourteen at the time, and they and I stayed in our home in suburban Maryland. It was not an easy time for any of us and, like any family breaking apart, each member paid a big price. Mine was a feeling of failure and disconnectedness, not unusual but very real nonetheless. Despite these feelings, I had to continue work and to provide as supportive an environment for the children as I could. I am sure my efforts left much to be desired, but they eventfully thrived anyway. Anita went on to Goucher College, got her M.S. in public health at the University of North Carolina, and later, before and while raising a family of three boys, earned her C.P.A. certification. Ever since her school days she has worked to support herself and her family, and she now is in the midst of a career at Medicare's central facility in Baltimore. Larry went to Cornell University, where he received an engineering degree in operations research, and then to Duke University, where he earned an M.B.A. degree. From Duke, he went to New York City and southern Connecticut areas, where he had considerable success working in several large businesses, the last as treasurer of an oil refinery company. Recently, he decided to try something he had long wanted to do, teach math in high school. Alongside his wife, Joy, he has been very involved in raising three children, a boy and two girls. So, if you have been counting, I am blessed with six grandchildren; the oldest (Aaron) is thirteen and the youngest (Seth) is six. And I better mention the others or I'll hear from them: Lee (twelve), Rachel (twelve), Hannah (ten), and Ken (ten).

By late 1985 both Anita and Larry were off and well ensconced in their college careers. There was little opportunity for further advancement where I was and, in any event, I felt the need for a new direction. I wanted to deal more directly with individuals and their personal legal problems, and I wanted to provide services to those who might otherwise not be able to afford them. So I left the area of utility law and began a third career working as an attorney for the Legal Counsel for the Elderly in Washington, D.C., an organization sponsored by the National Association of Retired Persons (NARP). I spent two satisfying and delightful years there, assisting indigent elderly persons with a wide variety of common legal matters, such as landlord-tenant issues, development of wills, obtaining public benefits, securing social security benefits, drafting guardian-ships and powers of attorney, etc. My colleagues at that office were very capable and generous with their assistance and advice, and they were committed to the population they were serving. I learned a great deal both from them and from my elderly clients. The work introduced me not only to a whole new arena of legal issues, but also to the local District of Columbia courts and administrative agencies.

My contact with the District of Columbia courts made me aware of other opportunities to provide legal services to those in need. This knowledge became useful when the budget for the Legal Counsel for the Elderly was cut and I, as the newest attorney in that office, had to be let go. The next and last phase of this third and final career was about to begin.

For the next seventeen to eighteen years, I was a solo law practitioner. I did a little corporate work and some divorce work during that period, but my primary interest was court-appointed cases. There were four main areas in which I worked.

The first, and most important in terms of time spent, number of cases handled, and emotional involvement, was that involving neglected and abused children. Under District of Columbia law, when a child, after some initial investigation by a social worker or the police, was deemed at risk of being neglected or abused, that child was brought in to the court to determine what, if any, steps were needed for his/her protection. When the child was brought before the court, attorneys were appointed to represent the child as well as each of the parents. Most often the child had been living with the mother, sometimes with a grandmother and rarely with a father. In the large majority of cases, fathers were missing and, under the law, efforts had to be made to locate them and advise them of their parental rights. There is a line of cases by the Supreme Court delineating broad constitutionally protected rights of parents to raise their own children. As with all such rights, there are limits also. A parent has no right, for example, to abuse, or neglect to provide the basic needs of his child. But the devil, as is so often the case, is in the details. Is a spanking abuse and if not, when does such physical activity become abuse? Is failure to send a child to school automatically neglect and if not, how frequently before it becomes so? The factual situations are endless, and that is where the attorneys and the courts come in.

In the hundreds of such cases I was involved in over the many years I was doing this work, I was most often appointed to represent the child(ren). In the others, I was appointed to represent the mother or, less frequently, the often-missing father. When appointed to represent the child, I had the title of guardian ad litem. As guardian it was my first task to learn as quickly as I could what the child's situation was and to help the court decide whether the child needed to be removed from his home pending final adjudication of the matter. This initial period in court was always very traumatic, both for the child and the mother, and that was particularly true if the court determined that the child should be removed. If there was a grandmother or aunt who was both reliable and interested, then she would be the court's first choice for placement of the child. If not, then a foster care placement was required.

My experience with foster care parents was generally good. At the very minimum, there was a sense of relief in moving a child from an abusive home into one that would at least be safe and supportive. I know there are abusive foster care parents that make the headlines at times, but the vast majority provided the basic support that was necessary. What they do often need is more training in dealing with emotionally damaged children.

Once in court, the child's case moves toward a determination of abuse or neglect by one of two routes: by trial, or by an agreement, signed by the parent(s) and attorneys and approved by the court, that the child was in fact neglected. As guardian it was my task to ensure that the child(ren) received all the educational, social, and other support services they needed. To do that, I would be in frequent contact with the assigned social worker. I would also visit the home in which the child was living (foster, relative, or at times still with a parent) once or twice a month. These visits brought me to almost every nook and cranny in the District, into areas where I otherwise never would have had an opportunity to see and learn about. It brought me into the most modest of homes as well as the occasional luxurious one. In addition to the home visits and interaction with social workers, I would periodically visit the schools for updates on "my" children and participate in education conferences concerned with the provision, as needed, of special-education services.

These cases could remain in the court system for years. Parents' ability to care for the kids often did not improve. An alternative permanent solution, such as adoption, was pursued, but often without success, despite increasing local effort and federal

mandates and money. Older children are particularly difficult
to place in adoptive homes. By law, children could—and some
did—remain under court supervision until they were twenty-
one.

Another line of cases in which I became involved were
criminal appeals. These involved adults who were found guilty
of major infractions in jury trials and who requested appeals
of their convictions. I would get involved because the attorney
appointed to represent such a defendant at the trial level would
not or could not handle the case on appeal; and the defendant,
by law, had the right to be represented by a lawyer on appeal.

My job was to review the case file, including the transcript of
the trial, and search for errors that may have been made at the
lower court level. From that search and a review of the relevant
case law and statutes, usually at least two or three appealable
issues could be developed. Those efforts were supplemented by
one or more interviews with the defendants, who were locked
up in local prisons. My first visit to such a prison was traumatic
as I stumbled my way through what seemed like endless security and identification procedures and gates in an overarchingly
gruesome environment. After the research and interviews I
would write the appellate briefs. Later I would need to prepare
a reply brief and then, usually, request and participate in oral
argument. The batting averages for success on such appeals are
quite low, and that was true of mine as well.

For some years, I participated in cases involving the mentally ill. These individuals had been apprehended most often
by police after some questionable behavior and brought to a
specialized institution, St. Elizabeth's Hospital. The law tried
to protect them from capricious official action in several ways.
One, perhaps the most important, was to ensure they had access
to the courts within twenty-four hours of their lockup to dem-
onstrate that there was no imminent danger of their hurting
themselves or others. Attorneys like myself were appointed to

represent them. My job initially was to rush over to St. Elizabeth's and interview my client to see if he/she wanted to appear in court the next day to contest being involuntarily hospitalized. Some were not clearheaded enough to discuss their options. Others had come from the streets, were tired and didn't want to object to a temporary stay. Yet others were unhappy with their state. Those I had to interview in detail and contact relatives or friends they might recommend as witnesses. We would appear in court the next day. The hearing was similar to a probable cause hearing in a criminal case. Many persons technically committed for care at the psychiatric hospital were released in a matter of days or weeks. Court reviews de novo of those commitments were available, but not often pursued. Periodic administrative reviews of long-term commitments are required.

Finally, I was involved in dozens of cases concerning the mentally retarded. These individuals were under the care of the District of Columbia because their families could not financially—and perhaps emotionally as well—care for them. My job was to ensure that they were adequately cared for and provided with as much opportunity as possible to develop the potential they had. To do that I had to visit their residences and daycare facilities quarterly. There were also administrative planning and review meetings and annual court reviews to prepare for and attend.

The clients ranged widely in their disabilities. A small number were categorized as mildly retarded, i.e., not too much below the seventieth percentile. As mentioned, the goal for them, as for others, was to provide services that would enable them to lead as normal and full a life as possible. One of my clients, for example, was able to obtain work and move into a subsidized apartment. It had taken years of services by D.C. social services to get him to that point.

A larger number were categorized as moderately retarded. For the most part, these individuals were ambulatory, could, with some supervision, care for their basic needs, and could interact with their caretakers and others. They lived in group homes, generally of six to eight persons who were similarly handicapped. The group homes were privately run under contract with the D.C. government. They varied greatly in the quality of both personnel and accommodations. The homes were staffed twenty-four hours a day, with at least two or three personnel in the mornings and evenings, when all their clients were in the home. Despite the voluminous developmental plans for each individual, I recall a dearth of programming and a maximum of television in those residences. During the weekdays, they went to various day programs, each one focused somewhat differently. The third grouping comprised individuals who were severely retarded and handicapped, both mentally and physically. They were wheelchair-bound and had minimum interaction with their environment, human or otherwise. All their basic needs had to be met by others. They, too, lived in group homes and went to day programs. They, especially, broke my heart when I visited them in facilities strewn all over the city.

But my heart did much better in other respects during those years. Most important was meeting and eventually marrying Martha Witebsky. Martha will someday write her own story, I hope. Born during the war in Germany, she witnessed plenty of destruction and experienced major deprivations. In 1958, she emigrated with her family to the States and slowly but surely learned English, finished high school, and eventually earned a college degree, while at the same time raising twin boys. Later she moved into patent translation work and recently retired as a translator from the U.S. patent office. Her two boys, Arthur and David, whom I've known since they were in middle school, have grown into fine young men, with careers and families of their own. Martha's passion in recent years—other than myself, of course—has been her four grandchildren.

I have been retired for over three years now. I do not miss

working, but it has required some thought and effort to ensure that my days are not only comfortable, but meaningful. I read a lot; I always have. I belong to book clubs, which meet monthly; and I attend classes in a lifelong learning program at Johns Hopkins University. I play at golf a few times a week; I travel some; and I tutor kids in reading at a local elementary school. I see my grandchildren as often as I can, for they are a joy and a challenge, and they add a spectrum of meaning and purposefulness to my life as I look both backward and forward.

It has been a long trip from Dorchester for me. My father and mother had even a longer trip to reach Dorchester, and my children and grandchildren will have their own lengthy journeys. And so it goes.

CHAPTER TWO

Arthur (Archie) Bloom

IT IS A CRYSTAL clear memory: my nickname of the time—
"Archie"—originated with Gordon Mirkin. He was fourteen
and I was thirteen and our two families, neighbors with abut-
ting dwellings—his family had a house, ours an apartment, one
of six in our building, located directly next door to theirs and
so we could speak across the alleyway from our bedroom windows—were about to share a summer rental in Nantasket Beach
on the South Shore of Boston, and Gordon wanted to put up
a sign with the names of the three children in the group: his,
mine, and his sister Janie's. But the name "Arthur," my proper
name, was somehow unacceptable to Gordon and since he was
doing the sign himself, he took the liberty of renaming me—I
was going to say "baptizing" me but there was nothing Chris-
tian about this—and he saw to the insertion of the new name
he had given without asking my permission. So, in the end, it
was, "Archie, Gordie, and Janie" in bold, black paint on a piece
of plywood, hanging from the front porch railing. The name
stuck, Gordon and I parted company soon thereafter, but my
group of teenage pals from that summer of 1947 continued to
call me Archie, and so I was to remain until well into Harvard,

and sometimes beyond—the human mind does not relinquish such catchy nomenclature with any ease.

Sometimes, as I sit sipping my morning espresso at the Café Luco on Boulevard Saint Michel here in Paris, up the street from our apartment and directly across from the Jardin du Luxembourg, I wonder how I found my way here. It is a long way, I can tell you, from Dyer Street in the Dorchester section of Boston to the *Quartier Latin* in Paris—a long, circuitous route, taking the better part of my seventy-five years. It was not a linear journey, but rather one filled with many sidetrips, some more interesting than others, to be sure, but overall a satisfying journey that has made up my life to date.

My neighborhood in Dorchester—the neighborhood that spawned me, in a real sense—was a small street between the very Jewish area at the junction of Norfolk and Morton Streets, where I went to elementary school, and the very Catholic Codman Square at the upper end of Norfolk Street. Dyer Street was comprised of a small number, perhaps twenty, of Jewish families living for the most part—Gordon Mirkin's house was an exception—in traditional, lower-middle-class, six-family Boston-style apartment buildings. The street was an island of Jewishness in a sea of Catholicism. Saint Matthew's Church was at the end of the street and around it lived a lot of poor Irish families who hated us Jews—the Spencer gang epitomized the youths with whom we daily sparred, sometimes with serious fights, their knives at our throats; and later, as we became teenagers, in more socially acceptable competitions like baseball and hockey up at the Dorchester town field of Dorchester High School. Even then, however, it was clear that the Catholics had been "sold a bill of goods" about the evil Jews who killed their savior, and I can still see Vinnie Pascarelli, one of the few kids of Italian origin in their group, skating at me with the blades of his hockey skates raised as he slid on the ice ostensibly to retrieve the puck but really to take down one of those Jews who saw to the death of Jesus. The purveyors of this line of hooey were the priests and nuns of Saint Matthew's, where most of the Irish kids, and Vinnie, had gone to elementary school. It was not uncommon for the holy ones to come charging out of the church as we Jewish kids crossed their playground on our way to Ginsberg's bakery or did other errands that took us towards Codman Square. They would, without hesitation, begin cursing us Jews, young though we were, for desecrating church lands with our presence, our Jewish presence. Still, despite all, I used to love the marvelously resonant bells of Saint Matthew's, which rang out the "Ave Maria" on many a Friday evening or Sunday morning. Got so I would even hum the tune, though almost silently, lest God should hear me and mistake my identity. That would have been only slightly less a problem than if my Grandmother Annie heard me.

After two innocuous years at the Frank V. Thompson Junior High School—innocuous educationally but personally traumatic because my parents did what Jewish couples rarely did in those days: they divorced—I moved on to the Boys Latin School over on Avenue Louis Pasteur in Boston, just off the treed Fenway and directly across the street from the Harvard Medical School. The Latin School was also adjacent to the Richardson House, the birthing center of the Peter Bent Brigham Hospital, and it was at the Richardson House that I was born. So going to the Latin School in the ninth grade was a serious homecoming, in a sense. I would sit in class sometimes and look out across the walkway to the Richardson House and say to myself, "Welcome back, Archie."

Life was very hard in those days, with Mother a wreck, trying to hold the family together while working as a secretary and trying to pay off dear old Dad's gambling debts—while Dad himself disappeared, only to appear from time to time at required court appearances for non-payment of child support or alimony. When Mother threw him in the Charles Street prison I was beside myself with a combination of rage at her, embarrassment for myself at having my old man in the hoosegow, and pity for him—he was a "nice guy" who just couldn't make it in the world. He was consumed with the ponies and the dog racing at Wonderland and had all he could do to avoid the guys to whom he owed money and his ex-wife who was intent on keeping him away from his son, his only child, so he would not be a "bad influence" on me.

Since I was the only kid on my block who went to the Latin School, the four years there held out the promise of some lonely times—it was terra incognita at a minimum. But I quickly made friends—lots of the guys were intimidated by the reputation of the school and by the masters who taught us—and kept blowing my trumpet, literally if feebly, but it got me into the marching band and kept me out of the otherwise obligatory military drill, which I was not at all into. I soon recognized that the divisions among my classmates ran along racial and ethnic grounds: the Irish kids came from South Boston (Southie) and Jamaica Plain, the Italian kids from East Boston (Eastadabost), the Jewish kids from Dorchester and Roxbury, and there was a rare Black from Roxbury and a rarer still Chinese from downtown. While the "melting pot" idea was then in vogue, the diversity of the school was, in fact, reflected in the separateness of its constituents—the Catholics became more Catholic, the Jews more Jewish, a kind of defense against the influence of the one upon the other.

I naturally and readily identified with the Jewish group, at least some of whom were part of the Dorchester-Roxbury B'nai B'rith AZA Chapter, #255, named for the famous Revolutionary War Jewish financier Haym Salomon. The chapter met on Sunday afternoons at the Hecht House, across from Franklin Park. The Catholic kids had their CYO (Catholic Youth Organization) centers, and the Jewish kids their Hecht House, where we could play basketball, have our meetings, go to day camp in the summers, hang out. I took to the AZA thing like a duck to water and it became for me, as for many of the thirty or forty members, the social and cultural center of our lives. When we weren't at the Hecht House we were partying at the houses of our fellow "Alephs," as members were called, later on organizing dances to which the B'nai B'rith girls from all around Boston were enthusiastically invited, doing "good works" in the Dorchester-Roxbury community, that sort of mixture of things. Mostly, however, we were becoming blood brothers—"tight," as the youth of today call it—inseparable in our lives outside of school, doing everything together. We dated the same girls—though not at the same time!—had our New Year's Eve parties together, looked after each other, shared our lives. When Irv Zola contracted polio and was in an iron lung, we were all there, trying to be supportive of Irving and his family; when Arthur Cohen's dad hanged himself in the Cohen's apartment over the bagel store, we all cried for Arthur, though a proper funeral was not allowed for religious reasons. In addition, we became known to our BLS comrades as this tight bunch of Jewish guys who, while mostly scholars and "machers," doers, still were not really to be messed with. We respected ourselves and they came to respect us, not so easy a matter for a Jewish group in those days—so soon after the Holocaust and just after the formation of the State of Israel.

Like ninety-nine other BLS students in our class, and like most, though not all, of my AZA brothers that year, I went to Harvard, the crowning achievement of a BLS career, and certainly a very big deal for a poor kid from Dorchester. As president of the famous *Cercle Français* of Max Levine at the Latin School, getting into Harvard was almost automatic—he had a pipeline—and with a scholarship to boot. I moved into the Harvard Yard, Hollis Hall, while most of my pals from the AZA commuted from home—I had a mother who urged me outward and a rich grand-uncle who offered to supplement my Harvard scholarship so long as I promised to become the first doctor in the family. By my sophomore year at Harvard I was sufficiently unsure about medicine as a career to so inform Uncle Bill, who promptly rescinded his supplement. I had visions of going to law school, so I could defend the poor who, it was clear, needed support in our legal system. Uncle Bill knew from lawyers and he was having none of that, so I was on my own. Mother did what she could and I had my Harvard scholarship as a base. I was determined not to leave Leverett House, to which I'd been assigned, and so I applied widely for additional monies—there are a lot of foundations wanting to help those who wish to help themselves. Realistically, there was no room for me "at home," the tiny one-bedroom apartment shared at that time by my mother and grandmother on Seaver Street in Roxbury, so returning to Mother's roof was not really an option. Anyway, living with them was no longer an option emotionally, as Mother and I often fought about my spendthrift ways. I worked summers in the Catskills—always an adventure—as a busboy, then as a waiter, and came to understand the ways of the itinerant student-worker bee.

At the Anderson Hotel and Country Club, a fleabag resort near Monticello, New York, I put in one especially grueling summer. I was the lone survivor among those who began the summer in June after my sophomore year, and I was blessed to have as my maître d', one Fred Witte, a Viennese émigré to New York, with long years of experience in the trade, in Europe, the City, and the mountains. Fred liked me and we shared that long, hard summer at the Anderson with relative aplomb, though the money was less than we both had hoped for. After a wickedly hard but financially rewarding Labor Day weekend, the last gasp of summer income, Fred came over to me, put his arm in brotherly fashion around my shoulder, and shared his wisdom, saying, "Arthur"—I was becoming Arthur in some circles—"you did a great job, but you are just not meant to wait on people, it is not in your nature. Find another, more suitable, line of work." I had never intended to become a professional waiter, which Fred knew, but I accepted Fred's words in the spirit in which he meant them, made it back to Boston for my junior year at Harvard, and really never looked back—except with gratitude for Fred's honesty and affection, and accuracy.

I debated throughout my four years at Harvard whether to go to medical school or graduate school in languages and literature. Having done my undergraduate thesis on Voltaire and his literary methods in attacking the Church, and having done so well at the stuff and liking it so, the conflict was natural between, on the one hand, the family's "given" that I was going to be a doctor, and, on the other hand, the dictates of my spirit, which led me in other directions. To hedge my bets, I applied both to medical school—after a very undistinguished series of pre-med courses at Harvard in which I had a solid C average!—and to graduate programs in comparative literature at Harvard and Columbia. I was accepted at both of the latter, with a lot of money especially from Columbia; but when the New York University School of Medicine accepted me I felt the call, packed my bags, and went to New York for science and medicine. In the end, with acceptances from medical and graduate schools in hand, I decided that I really did want to study medicine, that a career in Widener Library was just not physically active enough for me. But, the two-sided conflict was to last my lifetime. I had loved Harvard and had grown there intellectually and emotionally as I never could have imagined, but now was to become a medical person.

The graft was slow to take: At first I hated medical school. I was just too much into the arts to want to be stuck dissecting a cadaver at NYU, when MMA (the Metropolitan Museum of Art) and MOMA (the Museum of Modern Art) were now at my beck and call. I cut a lot of classes to see artsy movies—with

a predilection for French films, with the glorious Martine Car-
ole as "Nana," for example—and I went to Carnegie Hall more
often than was wise with regard to my medical school requirements, especially since my science background was weak to nil.
I just did not "get" the stuff for the longest time. Finally, Dean
Hubbard called me in, said the school had taken a chance on
me because I had done so well in my major at Harvard, and
maybe I should get down to work on biochemistry, physiol-
ogy, and the like. It was a moment of truth for me: did I really
want to do medicine or was I in New York to screw around? It
reminded me of a character in a Dirk Bogarde movie I saw at
the Exeter Theater in Boston years before, *Doctor in the House*,
in which this guy had a trust fund and could receive the annual
stipend only so long as he was a medical student—and so he
dutifully failed each year and received his stipend for the next!
I went on to barely pass my first-year exams, did materially
better in the second, though still no great shakes, and finally, as
the clinical years began, became a star on the wards at Bellevue,
taking care of patients, thinking acutely in terms of differential
diagnosis, and at last loving being a physician.

The era of DNA studies was just then beginning, and I got
very interested in genetics—Severo Ochoa, the great Brazilian
biochemist then at NYU, won the Nobel Prize for his work on
DNA polymerases, and he stimulated the faculty and upper-
level medical students to work on genetical questions. I did a
senior year research project on a rare metabolic disease, Maple
Syrup Urine Disease (MSUD), or branched chain ketoaciduria,
which afflicted young children, rendering them retarded before
killing them, and that took me down to eastern Carolina to
pursue a family with this rare disease. That, in turn, exposed me
to serious Southern segregation. The family I was studying, the
Jordans, were black, and there were separate hospitals, as well
as segregated rest rooms and "white only" restaurants in those
days, appalling to my liberal democratic sensibilities. I never

forgot the stories of the Underground Railroad told me by the patriarch of the Jordan family as we sat in the evenings on his porch, tales of how he had come up "north" from Georgia and settled his family in the Carolinas. I was, at last, able to "see" how medicine, genetics especially, and my fondness for the play of human emotions could be combined. I was at last a serious doctor, committed, respected and very content.

After doing a year as an intern at Bellevue in pediatrics, caring for the hordes of indigent little patients who lived on the Lower East Side of New York, barely having time for my own thoughts and needs, I decided to go elsewhere for residency. Johns Hopkins had a great department of general pediatrics, with a marvelous pediatric geneticist named Barton Childs on the faculty. I took the train to Baltimore, had an interview with him and with other distinguished pediatricians there, all of whom were interested in my MSUD genetic studies at Bellevue. Barton, who would later become my mentor and friend, handed me a piece of chalk and said, "Tell me what you did and what you found." I left at the end of that day elated that these great academic pediatricians found my research of interest, and hoping that I could somehow get a residency at that superb institution.

The telegram from Hopkins arrived soon thereafter, and I was thrilled. In July of 1961 I started the residency at Hopkins and my medical career was really launched. However, six months into the year, the Berlin crisis erupted and the army needed doctors. As we had been advised to get into a program that would enable us to be deferred, some weeks before the call-up I had applied to the U.S. Public Health Service for a commission and so could be activated by them instead of going on active duty with the U.S. Army. That took place shortly before January 1, 1962. The Public Health Service in Washington did not know what to do with me, suggested a tour with their radiological health group, and assigned me to the National Institutes of Health (NIH) in Bethesda to study human cytogenetics, with an eye on the developing interest in the chromosome-level effects of ionizing radiations. I duly spent two years at NIH, in the haven of a research lab, and published my first studies on the effects of X-rays on the chromosomes of human blood cell lymphocytes. To have a paper in the *New England Journal of Medicine* at that early stage of my career was a rich reward for my efforts.

At the end of my tour, the PHS suggested I might want to remain on active duty while completing my pediatric residency at Hopkins, and I readily agreed—I had one child and another en route by then so the thought of returning to the poverty-level salary ($1,800 per year) of a Hopkins resident was not appealing. I returned to Baltimore and the rigors of clinical pediatrics at Johns Hopkins Hospital—thirty-six hours on, twelve hours off—with two years owing to the PHS at the end of it. The Hopkins years were wonderful, with a degree of excellence and pride unlike any I had experienced since my Harvard days. But the question rapidly became, what next? I was not, as Fred Witte would have recognized, cut out for the practice of pediatrics—too many neurotic mothers to tend to—so that was not really an option. I was a research pediatrician, specializing, or wanting to specialize, in genetic diseases of children.

I had a plumb lab position waiting for me at NIH in the laboratory of biochemical genetics of Chris Anfinsen, who would later also win the Nobel. But I just could not will myself back to the Bethesda suburbs—after Hopkins I wanted an adventure, like the Peace Corps or something similar. However, one did not simply turn down a treasured position in Anfinsen's lab, and when I told Anfinsen that I had decided to go to Japan to do genetics, he refused to discuss my decision with me and never spoke to me again.

But Japan was well worth any such price. The Public Health Service sent a few docs each year to Hiroshima and Nagasaki, and the PHS thought my training at NIH in the emerging field of human cytogenetics made me well-suited to ratchet up the studies of the A-bomb survivors, which were waiting to be done. I built a chromosome laboratory there, under the aegis of the Atomic Bomb Casualty Commission (ABCC), which was later to become the Radiation Effects Research Foundation (RERF), spent three instead of the obligatory two years, and along with my Japanese colleagues, made major discoveries regarding the induction by the radiations of the atomic bombs of chromosomal abnormalities in the blood cells of survivors. Importantly, we also demonstrated the absence of chromosomal abnormalities in their offspring, a source of no little comfort to the survivors and to the rest of us.

Japan was a pivotal experience both scientifically and personally. I produced a series of papers on atomic radiation effects on human chromosomes, became known by colleagues around the world for this work, and my career was "made." Personally, the years there were yet more rewarding: I came to love Japanese music, pottery, Noh theater, painting and architecture—and literature, above all the literature. I was dependent on the translations, of course, but they were very good, and through them I became familiar with Mishima, Kawabata, Abe, and others. When Yukio Mishima committed *hara kiri,* I was bereft: never sympathetic to his nationalistic politics but always attuned to his brilliance as a novelist, I spent years thinking about why the master had done himself in. I read a lot, played Japanese koto—the thirteen-stringed harp-like instrument made of pawlonia wood that was played while seated on the floor—and traveled throughout Japan and East Asia generally. I became a serious Japanophile, with interest in China as well. Nonetheless, I felt obliged to return to the States: first, I needed to "succeed" as a scientist in my native land—as an American I could never really be a part of the Japanese scientific establishment and would always an outsider; and second, my two marvelous, curly-headed daughters were the constant object of unwanted attention, looked upon as "monsters" among their exclusively Japanese nursery school classmates, and as foreign oddities in the neighborhood—not a very desirable way to grow up.

In returning to the U.S. I had a choice: I could have gone back to Hopkins, where Barton offered me a place in his lab; or, alternatively, establish my own lab at the University of Michigan in Ann Arbor as an assistant professor. Michigan had a very distinguished department of human genetics and I opted for the autonomy of my own operation. Son Bob was born in Ann Arbor and the birth of a first son gave me great joy. I had PhD students—from the U.S., of course, but also from Korea, Japan, Finland—and medical students, and developed a serious program in in vitro experimental genetic studies, especially revolving around the human lymphocyte, with its interesting capacity to survive forever once transformed by virus, allowing a wide range of studies of the human genome to be done. I had excellent colleagues, was promoted to associate professor with tenure, did clinical work which I valued, and mostly enjoyed Michigan and the Middle West. I was not, however, of the mind that Michigan would be my final professional resting place. Thus, when the call came to go to Columbia as a full professor, in the departments of pediatrics and human genetics, I accepted with excitement.

Soon after arriving in New York—where I was utterly delighted to be—my personal life fell apart. My penultimate wife and I had had troubles for many years, and after heroic efforts to keep it together, I decided to leave, move in to New York City, and see the kids on weekends and midweek, in order to prevent everyone's life from totally disintegrating, so great was the tension in the household. The divorce was not amicable, but my sense of relief was enormous—counterbalanced, of course, by the pain of the children. But I was sure that I had to leave and thus the certainty of the wisdom of the change made it manageable. I got a better life; the kids were able to live theirs without the daily anger, rage really, of two parents who had come to dislike one another; and the ex-, well, her life was then up to her.

For many years Columbia and New York City served as the bases of my life. I had pride in my professorship at a wonderful university where my colleagues were, if not always pleasant, at least almost always smart; we did grand things in the lab research-wise; I made rounds on the wards at Babies Hospital and at other Columbia-affiliated hospitals, teaching pediatrics and genetics to bright House Staff and medical students; I served on distinguished NIH study section review committees; I was elected to the board of directors of national and state-wide organizations, such as the American Society of Human Genetics and the March of Dimes Birth Defects Foundation; and I put in lots of time coaching my children's softball and baseball teams in Scarsdale, spending most every weekend with the three of them until they got older and began opting out from time to time. I saw Karen satisfactorily into Barnard, then Michelle into Harvard and Bob into the University of Arizona via Syracuse University. We were close and remain close and mostly loving, really loving, to this day.

I loved the life of the City, too. The cultural life, the social *rondes,* the privacy when I wanted/needed it. The pulse of the City throbbed in my veins, and I was delighted to be a distinguished professor in New York, with a buck or two in my pocket, a lot of ego-massaging daily, and good health to boot. Mother would come down from Boston from time to time, and urge me without success to join her at the opera—that graft finally "took" years later—but we did other things together, and I shared my personal life with several interesting women, and others I could have done without. I had a project down in the Cayman Islands, too, documenting the extent of the genetic diseases in that inbred population, and would go down to the

Caribbean for months at a time, often with the kids in hand, to work and play, mainly on Grand Cayman Island. Columbia was not entirely sympathetic to my efforts and my absences, and the situation was aggravated further by my opening a commercial genetics laboratory with the twenty percent of my time allowed to faculty for such non-university-based activities. When I refused to give Columbia a percentage ownership in the company, which was financed by a venture capital group, the unpleasantness increased.

Further, I had, prior to this time, begun to grow disquiet with my academic life in medicine, and wanted increasingly to sit quietly and write—not science or medicine but fiction. I took courses in the writing program on the Morningside campus of Columbia and somehow felt happy doing those papers. It was for me a joy to be able to use the other side of my brain; I was feeling stifled at the College of Physicians and Surgeons, not particularly anyone's fault, just a feeling I was not sufficiently self-expressed. I had enjoyed medicine and genetics, but I began to grope for something more, something other.

About this time, in the summer of 1981, I met and seriously took up with Deborah Schwarz, my now wife of twenty-eight years. Deborah had studied economics at Syracuse and law at Harvard Law School in a combined program with the Russian Research Center, before departing for Columbia and art history. We met en route to China—I was medical director of a genetics group, she was our Chinese-speaking guide—and we have been sharing life ever since. After we married, in 1982, we bought a weekend house in Columbia County, New York, just south of Albany, nestled in the Berkshires. That became our spiritual home, with its gorgeous views of the Catskill sunsets, its frigid snow-covered winters, and the ambience we both needed to breathe deeply. I took a leave of absence from Columbia, got a job in Pittsfield at the Berkshire Medical Center, where I established my own institute, the Environmental Health Institute, took additional writing courses at the New York State Writers' Institute, and finally, in 1988, severed my ties to Columbia University. Curiously, there was little if any pain involved; mostly I was relieved to be cast (somewhat) adrift. Deborah turned to fashion design and built her own business in the Berkshires.

The institute was my own creation and I worked hard to establish its funding, which, with the inestimable help of Congressman Silvio Conte of the first congressional district of Massachusetts, I did. We published, with superb genetical colleagues from around the country and beyond, numerous books and papers on the genetic risks and health effects of environmental exposures, the genetic predisposition to disease in the face of environmental agents, and finally on the relationship between environmental factors and degenerative diseases of the brain.

With the impending arrival of baby Noah in 1987, Deborah and I bought a less isolated house, a Georgian with a lot of land on rural Route 22 in nearby Austerlitz, which became the center of our very happy lives for several years thereafter. Deborah designed and sold dresses at her shop in Chatham, New York; my institute was generating lots of good books and scientific articles; and Prince Noah was toddling about, under the watchful eyes of his Grandmother Ethel from Boston. With the fall of the Berlin Wall in 1989, and the extreme environmental contamination of Eastern Europe, I saw a potential role for an extension of my institute into that region of the world. After my Marco Polo journey across Europe to assess what needed done, I formed an international scientific committee on health and the environment, consisting primarily of researchers from Eastern Europe and the United States. We elected to base the new group in Paris, for ease of access to research funds from Western Europe and the States, and, truth be told, because I adored Paris, have always adored Paris. Deborah and I sold our home in Austerlitz, and with Noah, age five, and grandmother, age eighty-five, in hand, we took an Air France flight on a snowy winter's night at the end of December 1992 from Newark to Paris and began our new life abroad.

The Eastern European project died a slow death: I took offices for us at the Hôpital Saint Louis in the tenth arrondissement of Paris, where the scientific counsel *(conseil scientifique)* of the hospital was very enthusiastic about our environmental work. The Hôpital Saint Louis was founded in the fifteenth century as a leprosarium and a hospital for bubonic plaque patients. Our offices were in the old part of the hospital, where such patients were housed long ago, and while the offices themselves were a decaying catastrophe, they overlooked one of the most charming courtyards in Paris, which made life very pleasant. My group and I tried over several years to raise serious sums of money for the work that needed done in Russia, the Ukraine, Hungary, the Czech Republic, Slovakia, et alia. The contamination of the air, water and soil from chemical plants in those countries was enormous, as was the radioactivity that had spewed forth from aged and poorly built nuclear power plants—viz. Chernobyl. The problem was that scientists themselves were very poorly paid, their labs inadequate, and, most of all, the governments in these countries did not really want to know about the health effects of their environmental pollutions, because if it became known what those effects were, they would have had to update the technology and clean up the sites, neither of which, in that post-Soviet era, they could afford to do. And so few willing investors could be found; the black hole that was Eastern and Central Europe was just too overwhelming. (George Soros, for example, put over $100 million dollars into the support of scientists and laboratories in Russia and the Czech Republic, with said money producing little of lasting impact in those countries).

At any rate, I had other ideas beyond the resurrection of Eastern European science. I had taken writing courses at Columbia and thereafter (I was then, and remain now, skeptical about the teaching of the craft, though Americans seem to believe in it, while the French do not) and now used those courses to refocus my thinking, my desires for the future. So when we got to Paris, where writers and writing are much respected, and with the attendant freedom I felt in being in a country other than my own, the freedom for me to be other than a physician, to be other than what I had been to this point in my life, I began, once the Eastern European study petered out, to write seriously. Day after day, in our modest apartment in the sixteenth arrondissement, after walking Noah to the local *école élémentaire*, I would sit at my desk, with a view of the one tree in our courtyard, computer on, writing the first non-scientific book I had ever composed, wondering if I could really do this. I wrote about what I knew, turning my thoughts about Paris into an essay on what life was like for an American ex-pat living in Paris. "Tales of an American Emigré in Paris" was published in Paris by the Société des Ecrivains in late 2000. With no marketing of this English-language book by the Parisian publisher, sales were modest, but family and friends seemed to enjoy it, which gave me pleasure. And, out of this process, I became, I felt, a writer.

We moved out of Paris in 2002 to Saint Germain en Laye, about fifteen miles west, in order for Noah to attend the Lycée International, where as a member of the American Section he would be forced to read and write English at a higher level than in the previous schools he had attended in Paris. His spoken English had always been excellent, but his written English to that point was, well, mediocre. But once he began the equivalent of tenth grade at the Lycée he developed quickly into the kind of native English-speaker and writer he would need to be to compete successfully for admission to the best colleges in the U.S., which is where he always wanted to go.

Soon after our move to Saint Germain en Laye, the first visitors from my Haym Salomon days came to France for a gathering: Paul Rosenthal, Marty Mintz, Zummie Katz, Arnie Abelow, Don Orenbuch, Ray Leiter, Jerry Davidow, all with wives, spent several days under our aegis in and about Paris and Saint Germain en Laye, and then three days in Normandy at our *moulin*, seeing the war memorials and the landing beaches. That week resuscitated, after more than fifty years, our general interest and enthusiasm for the group, and additional reunions have recently followed, in Cambridge (June 2006) and Florida (March 2007).

I continued my writing, and began laboring over my first novel, *Citron's Sonata* (Athena Press, London). Again, I was unsure about my ability to write fiction, but something interesting happened as I got further into the book: After perhaps fifty pages of what was threatening to be largely an autobiographical work, the character I had created—Harry Citron, professor of literature and a well-recognized literary critic, especially known for his work on Camus and other French writers of the twentieth century— became other than Arthur Bloom, took on a life of his own and lived not my life but his. Had his own women, his own children, traveled where he wanted to travel, and ultimately died his own death. The book was published in the summer of 2007, and I have done readings from it, most recently here in Paris at the Village Voice Bookstore under the auspices of both the bookstore and the Harvard Club of France. There seems to be a reasonable body of readers who like the work, and I certainly enjoyed the writing. I have a friend who believes that a book that no one reads is like a scream in the woods that no one hears. I don't agree, since the writing per se is a complex act—largely pleasurable for me at this time, and the book, like the scream, stands by itself. Still…one wants his words read and appreciated, preferably within his lifetime, and I think the reaction to this first novel has been very satisfying.

The children—they'll always be children even though well grown—have been a complex source of joy, delight and anxiety over the years. Karen has been installed at John Hancock in Boston for over ten years now and is a residential expert in information technology. Michelle is a professor of comparative literature and French at the University of California Riverside, where she teaches and writes articles and books of her own. Son Bob, of great athletic prowess and psychological insight, works in physical fitness and training, most recently with older persons in Florida, where he is based. Son Noah finished his undergraduate work at Harvard (Harvard '09) in the department of art and architecture, also having spent four years writing and editing on the staff of the *Harvard Crimson*. He is now an investment banker in London. My four children are very different each from the others, but I love them for their struggles as well as their successes.

As for Deborah and I, we adore France and will continue to live both in Paris and the United States, as she grows her English-language training company internationally. Innumerable family members and friends have died during our years in Paris—parents, aunts and uncles—and that has been very painful indeed. Makes us reconsider, from time to time, the decision to be ex-pats, but the values here are our values and so we move easily between Paris and Boston/New York.

For my part, I treasure sitting peaceably in my local cafés, sipping an espresso in the morning, having a beer or another coffee in the afternoon, and wine with dinner, writing in between or in the wee hours of the morning. I walk a lot, especially the streets of the fifth arrondissement, where we live—the *Quartier Latin*—and enjoy the feeling of being in a place where the smells and sights and experiences are constantly a revelation, where there is always something new to discover, to learn. It is, indeed, a long way from Dorchester and my roots in the AZA, but somehow this life seems a logical extension of that life, all of a piece.

CHAPTER THREE

Irwin Kabler

The Storm

ONE OF MY EARLIEST memories is of the rain beating down so heavily on my bedroom window that I thought the glass would break. The wind swirling around outside sounded like a freight train roaring right into my room. I was very frightened and so were my mom and dad as we all huddled together in their room. What we did not know was that we were right in the middle of the 1938 hurricane that devastated New England without any advance warning. There was no TV then, with the frightening announcements of impending doom, nor was there much of an early-warning system on the radio or in the newspapers to alert the public to what was coming. We just sat, waited and prayed for the storm to blow over.

The next morning we awoke to bright sunshine, a beautiful blue sky and a mild breeze. Looking out from my bedroom window, everything looked the same, with no indication of what had transpired the night before. However, when I walked around the corner to my grandmother's house and checked the backyard, everything was totally destroyed. The beautiful pear trees that gave us such delicious fruit were lying on the ground, my grandmother's prized grape vines were gone and my little patch of a garden no longer existed. These memories are still very vivid in my mind, as the storm made such a traumatic impact.

Family

My mom and dad were first-generation Americans, born in the greater Boston area. Both were hard workers all their lives. Dad had a small jewelry repair shop in the Jewelers Building, located at 387 Washington Street in Boston, and somehow managed to eke out a small living. We were poor, but never knew it, as everybody in our neighborhood was also poor. Mom had worked for a cigar and tobacco company until I was born and then became the proverbial stay-at-home wife and mother. We had a very strong nuclear family, with almost all the aunts, uncles and cousins living within a short distance from each other, centered around the matriarch grandmother of the family, who lived at 48 Wildwood Street, Dorchester. My maternal grandparents came to the United States from Riga, Latvia, via Leeds, England, and somehow settled in East Boston. My grandmother ran a small convenience-type store, and my grandfather was a tailor. I never knew my grandfather, but I was named for him after he passed away, which was a tradition in those days. My brother, born five years after me, was named for my paternal grandfather.

My grandparents then moved to Wildwood Street in Dorchester, which was nothing but a dirt road, and set about raising a family of two sons and four daughters. My grandmother was extremely active in helping to establish Temple Beth Hillel on Morton Street and the small "shul" on Woodrow Avenue She also ran the "mikvah" on the other side of Wildwood Street. During World War II, she had all the neighborhood women in her house, with their sewing machines, making bandages and packages for the soldiers. Her proudest achievement was a plaque signed by President Harry S. Truman honoring her work for the American Red Cross. As you can imagine, she was a very strong woman and definitely the matriarch of the family, so that all activities and holidays centered around her home, including the usual Saturday night dinners and get-together. The men would play cards, the women mahjongg, and my dad would play the piano. He never had a lesson in his life, but if anyone just hummed or sung a tune, he could play it. I understand that he also played the drums in an orchestra when he was young, but unfortunately he never passed on that musical gene to me.

My paternal grandparents lived at 12 Nightingale Street in Dorchester. I am told that the origins of the Kabler family were in Spain, and the family moved to Germany during the Inquisition. Much later in time, my grandparents moved to the United States. My father was a blue-eyed, fair-skinned blond, who somewhere along the line inherited the Aryan gene but never passed it on to me or my brother. My father's family consisted of three sisters and four brothers, whom I did not know very well. What we did not know was that he was also supporting his mother and a sister on the small income he earned. Somehow, we all made it. We would visit them occasionally on Sunday, but not too often. When we did visit I would play with my cousins and a boy next door who was also visiting his grandparents. Little did we know that many years later he and I would end up as roommates at Tufts and become members of the same fraternity. We are still friendly today and see each other occasionally in Florida.

Dorchester

Living in Dorchester in the forties was like living in a *shtetl*. Despite the fact that the war was raging in Europe and the Pacific, everything was fairly normal, with the exception of the ration books for food and other necessities. My dad was too old for the army so he was a volunteer air raid warden, with a heavy steel helmet, a nightstick and an armband. I still have those souvenirs of the war. We did not have to worry about gasoline coupons as we could not afford a car, so we distributed our coupon allotment to family members who were lucky enough to have a car.

Life as a young kid was going to public schools, which meant a walk of about 500 yards. I made many friends there, and they were all Jewish, as the school was about ninety-nine-percent Jewish in the ghetto. The local schools actually had to close for all of the Jewish holidays, major and minor, as no one attended class. My best friend was Josh, and because of the spelling of our last names he sat directly behind me for all the years we spent at *cheder*. The Dorchester–Mattapan Hebrew School was about 200 yards from our apartment and required five days of attendance, Sunday through Thursday, not including Sabbath services, which we were also expected to attend. In the younger grades, Hebrew school hours were right after dismissal from public school, 4:00 p.m. to 6:00 p.m., and 11:00 a.m. to 1:00 p.m. on Sunday. The older grades went from 6:00 p.m. to 8:00 p.m. weekdays and from 9:00 a.m. to 11:00 a.m. on Sunday. In our family you were expected to excel in both public and Hebrew school or Grandma would take you to task. I had my Bar Mitzvah with Rabbi Jacobsen officiating at Temple Beth Hillel, followed by a formal party at the Aperion Plaza (owned by the Jacobsen family) on Warren Street in Roxbury. Don't ask how my parents were able to afford such a lavish party, but they did, and enjoyed every minute of it with their friends and family, some of whom I did not know.

One of my uncles managed some apple orchards in Lincoln, and some other towns in the area. It was great fun to ride with him in his Diamond "T" truck (which I don't think had any springs) to go apple-picking or to deliver the boxes to the local markets. He also had a Ford coupe with a rumble seat that I would pile into with my cousins for a ride through the Sumner Tunnel to visit his family in Lynn. I spent many a Sunday on Fisherman's Beach checking out the girls.

Even though we did not own a car, I got my license at the age of sixteen like all the other guys. I was then able to work for another uncle whenever he needed me, making deliveries, cleaning out the stock room and doing all sorts of other errands. He must have trusted me, as he had me drive him to Brooklyn, New York, just shortly after I got my license. That was a thrill and a half, as the only road at that time was Route 9, which wove its way west through almost every small town in Massachusetts. I must have been a good driver, as he would let me use the car on Saturday nights for special dates.

Sports

Summers were spent wearing our PF Keds black high-tops, playing all sorts of unorganized games in the streets, school yards, Norfolk playground or Franklin Field. We spent long hours playing stickball with a "pinkie" ball and some mother's broomstick. Most games were played in the school yard of the Bradford Elementary School, and strict records were kept of home runs over the fence. One hundred twenty to 150 were about average for a summer season. Once the ball split in half, it then became a game of "half ball" until enough money could be found to buy a new "pinkie." Sometimes a "pimple" ball was an acceptable substitute. Basketball in the school yard was also popular—the hoop was a peach basket with the bottom cut out, attached to the fire escape.

Another great game played in the Bradford school yard was "boxball," which was played on an invisible diamond either with or without a pitcher or catcher. The intent was to hit the ball with your hand or fist and have it bounce within the diamond, but below knee level. If the hit ball ever got through the left side, it was usually a home run as it ran the total length of the school yard. The right side was basically a chain link fence, so the ball was usually in play and most times was just a single. This game was also played by other groups in other school yards, and inter-school-yard games were sometimes played. As we grew older and spent weekends at Nantasket Beach, to the south of Boston, a diamond was drawn in the hard sand at low tide and the game was played until dark. Ray and I became good summer friends during those summers in Nantasket until we both headed off to different colleges and did not see each other again.

As soon as the weather got cold, I would put a small jar filled with water on our back porch. As soon as it froze and broke, I knew it was cold enough to go ice skating. Almont playground was one of our favorite places to skate and play pick-up games of hockey. Not too many Jewish kids played hockey but that did not seem to be a problem. Somehow, I scrounged together enough money to have a pair of hockey skates, gloves, a stick, a puck and shin guards. That was all the equipment that was needed to play. It was a long walk from Morton Street via Norfolk Street to Blue Hill Avenue and then to Almont Street right after school and we played hockey until it was too dark to see the puck. I would then take the streetcar back to Morton Street and home to do homework.

High School Years

As we grew older, the gang dispersed to different junior and then senior high schools. I enjoyed junior high at the Frank V. Thompson, worked hard, played baseball and basketball, and played drums in the band. When it was time to select a high school, I probably surprised a lot of people, including myself, by attending Roxbury Memorial, rather than Boston Latin. That decision still puzzles and obsesses me, but I made the best of the situation, worked hard, played basketball and baseball with my friend Skip, became captain of the band and class valedictorian. I did not play hockey in high school, as the games were usually on Saturday mornings and I had to work.

Back in those days, Boston had a schoolboy parade downtown in the spring in which all high schools and junior highs participated. As captain of the band, I did not have to play an instrument but marched proudly beside the band announcing when we were approaching a reviewing stand so we could play the "Washington Post March" over and over again since it was the only piece we knew really well. It worked, as our band came in second to Boston Latin School in my senior year. After the parade was over, we stayed downtown at the Boston Common, met our girlfriends and had a wonderful time. Ice cream sundaes at Bailey's on Tremont Street were a treat, with chocolate sauce dripping all over the dish and saucer.

As soon as I became sixteen, I obtained a work permit and my dad found me a job at a men's store called Howard Clothes, located at 342 Washington Street in downtown Boston. It was right next door to a famous Boston landmark called Raymond's. A good friend of mine worked there so we tried to have lunch and coffee together. I started out working all day Saturday and after school Monday and Wednesday evenings until 8:00 p.m. wrapping bundles. Eventually, I progressed to selling shirts, ties, etc., and then to suits and coats. I was very fortunate that I could always count on working there any time I had a high school or college vacation. That job helped put me through college. During the summer, I would take my lunch break and walk over to the Boston Common bandstand on Tremont Street and eat my brown bag lunch listening to a concert. Times were good back then.

Social activities usually centered around the Hecht House on American Legion Highway. I joined Haym Salomon AZA, which had its meetings there on Sundays afternoons, and I became friendly with a totally different group of guys. Most of them went to Boston Latin and they all had great ambitions for themselves, with academic achievements high on the list. A highlight event each year was the Haym Salomon-sponsored scholarship-fund dance at the Totem Pole in Newton. This became a much-anticipated social event every February school vacation. I find it amazing how this group of guys have matured from teenagers to men and have managed to stay in touch with one another over the years and really care for each other. It is truly a pleasure to be included.

I also joined a sports club at the Hecht House, played pool and basketball in the gym, where three of the four walls were out of bounds. As a result, lots of black-and-blue bruises were seen after most games. Tuesdays, Thursdays and Saturday nights were dance nights, with a jukebox full of the latest music. It cost a quarter to get into the dance and have your hand stamped. If my homework was done, I tried to go, but sometimes it was a little difficult since I was then working at Howard Clothes. It was a tight but manageable schedule and somehow I came through unscathed and was ready to head off to college.

After synagogue services on the High Holidays, the afternoons were spent along The Wall at Franklin Field, where kids of all ages, dressed in their finest clothes, socialized. The Ames Brothers (a singing group from Dorchester), would entertain at the corner of Talbot and Blue Hill Avenues. There exists today a Franklin Field Association, mainly of retirees living in Florida, which publishes a monthly online newsletter reminiscing about the good old days. Every February there is a large reunion in Ft. Lauderdale, Florida, of approximately 500 people from Dorchester, Mattapan and Roxbury.

Sundays in the summer were spent at the Talbot Bowladrome bowling, socializing, hanging out or bumming a ride to Nantasket Beach rather than trying to hitch a ride. Try explaining this lifestyle to your kids today. They will probably look at you as if you were crazy. It was just another time in another place.

College

I had always been good working with my hands, excelled in math and science, and decided to become an engineer. My dad always said I would become an engineer as he proudly examined the latest Erector Set creations I made as a kid. I applied to a number of colleges but realized that I could never afford them. Tufts College (it did not become a University until two years later) became my college of choice. After applying to Tufts, I received a phone call to meet the dean and was excited since Tufts was close to home, reasonably affordable and I could continue to work in Boston part time. My first semester tuition bill was all of $325, which was a lot of money to me then since my dad could only afford to give me $5.00 a week toward school to supplement the scholarships and loans that I managed to obtain. I was accepted by the dean and I started classes the following September in the electrical engineering department. That turned out to be a bad decision as I had a very difficult but passable freshman year. I then transferred into the mechanical engineering department as a sophomore, was much happier, but had a lot of additional courses to make up. I attended class from 8:00 a.m. until noon, had lunch at the fraternity house and went back to the labs from 1:00 p.m. until 4:30 p.m. Monday through Friday. There were also classes on Saturday mornings from 8:00 a.m. until noon. We certainly got a lot of school for our money back then. If I had a date for a Saturday afternoon football game, one of my fraternity brothers would have to pick her up for me.

My social life revolved around the AEPi fraternity, which somehow I was able to afford by working in Boston and at the foundry, which still existed on the engineering campus. I was a teaching assistant there and learned more about metallurgy than I was able to teach. The food at the fraternity house was considerably better than in the school dining halls and the social activities were great. I chose not to live in the fraternity house as it was noisy and I needed a quiet place to study to catch up with my additional classwork. Fortunately, I found a small apartment around the corner from the fraternity house, which I shared with another engineering student, and it worked out just fine. It was at a Friday night fraternity party that I met a young lady from Brookline who was attending Forsyth (a school for dental hygienists), which held some of their academic classes on the Tufts campus. I pursued her diligently in my spare time, and between classes we would meet on campus. After awhile, she accepted my fraternity pin, a custom on campus back then. We became engaged and married after she finished school. We moved to Norwich, Connecticut, which was just twelve miles up the Thames River from New London, and rented a four-room house for all of $79 per month and began married life.

Working Career

After graduating *cum laude* from Tufts, I went to work for the Electric Boat Division of General Dynamics Corporation in Groton, Connecticut, as an engineer in the research and development department. I worked on a number of R&D projects before transferring to the radiation analysis section and began to work on various nuclear submarine proposals. Work in the shipyard was fascinating, as the nuclear submarine fleet was rapidly expanding, and it was exciting to see a new ship that you worked on launched and commissioned into the United States Navy. Most of my work was spent designing, building and testing the nuclear reactor compartments, which provided propulsion and electrical power to the ships. The work schedule was 24/7 at the shipyard during the Korean War. I was exempt from military service as I received a deferment because of the classified work I was doing in the shipyard.

We had two boys while living in Norwich, and I attended the University of Connecticut part time nights and earned a master of science degree in engineering and an MBA degree. After ten years of living in Connecticut, my wife wanted to move back to the Boston area. We bought a house in Framingham, and I went to work for the Polaroid Corporation in Cambridge. The first day on the job, I did not get home until 10:00 p.m., as those were the glory days of a high-flying Polaroid.

I worked a few years as an engineer helping to build the film-assembly machinery that made the very complicated film for the cameras. These machines were at least 150 feet long and consisted of a number of separate stations bolted together. Raw materials, such as the film negative, the film positive, batteries, chemical pods, etc. began their journey through various sections of the machine to be assembled into finished film packages. After the machines were completed and tested, they were taken apart, section by section, and transported to Waltham, Mexico or Scotland, where they were reassembled and put into production. My job was to coordinate the manufacturing, contracting and purchasing of the hundreds of components that had to be ready on time to assemble these very large, complicated machines. It was an exciting and fun job experience.

Through the fifties and sixties Polaroid was expanding at an enormous pace and required people with analytical skills and a background in business and finance. I was selected to join the newly established finance division and started a new phase of my working life, with numerical and financial analysis as opposed to creating some kind of physical product. I worked on preparing the corporate balance sheets, profit and loss statements, materials for the monthly board of directors meeting, audit reviews and various other financial requirements and disciplines. I was then assigned to the corporate payroll department and shortly became the senior financial manager. At that time, Polaroid had over 20,000 employees working worldwide that had to be paid accurately and on time. In addition, all federal, state and local payroll taxes were required to be prepared, paid and delivered on time so that no penalties were incurred. All of this was done utilizing a very old, in-house payroll system. I organized a team of in-house systems analysts and payroll specialists to completely design and prepare a new in-house corporate system, with the flexibility to make changes quickly and accurately to conform to any new government regulations as well as any new human relations benefit changes. This task was completed in a comparatively short time and became respected (and maybe even envied) by other companies that prepared their payroll and taxes in-house. The system was so unique that we were able to completely balance the financial results after each payroll run, so there were no surprises at year end when it was time to prepare W-2 forms for all employees. We then became known as the first company in the country to have W-2 forms ready for their employees when they returned to work after the New Year's holiday. We also inherited three separate payroll time periods—weekly, twice a month and monthly. This was cumbersome and expensive to maintain, so the system was changed to pay all employees every other week (bimonthly). This change saved the company a large amount of money, especially when most employees then had their pay directly deposited into their bank accounts.

Married Life

We had a daughter while living in Framingham, joined the temple and lived the middle-class life of dinners with friends, socializing and watching our children progress through school and grow into young adults. Like many others, little did I realize that our marriage was slowly falling apart; soon we were divorced, after seventeen years of marriage. I spent a few years as a very unhappy bachelor, living with some cousins for a short period, and then I set up my own bachelor pad. I dated a number of women, none seriously, stayed very close to my kids and went to every band concert, school play and football game. It was at a birthday party for my friend and boss that the wife of a friend of mine from Dorchester realized that the woman I was with was not my wife. She checked with the hostess and called me very early the next morning to tell me about her divorced sister, who lived in Marblehead. Marblehead was the other side of the world for me, but she was very persistent and insisted that I call her sister. That was the best and most opportune phone call that I ever made, and she and I started dating as often as possible. I used every excuse possible to get to Marblehead and even went to court in Salem representing Polaroid (a job usually assigned to one of my employees) whenever I had the chance, and then spent a few lunch dates in Marblehead. It took a lot of convincing, but after about a year of dating she finally agreed to get married and has become the love of my life and my true soulmate.

After we were married, I moved from Framingham into her home in Marblehead with her two children. Since I had three kids, we had quite a brood when they were all together. Fortunately, the kids interacted very well, which made things much easier for my new wife and me. We expanded the back porch to accommodate the large family and added solar panels to the roof and a very large hot water tank. I commuted to work from Marblehead; my wife was a school adjustment counselor and then a teacher in Lynn. We watched all of our children grow into young adults, get married and have families of their own. The years passed very quickly and I can only say that after being married a second time, for thirty-four years and counting, these have been the best years of my life. I can only give all the credit to my wife for putting up with me.

Meanwhile, over the years Polaroid started to decline as a viable long-term company, as camera technology changed rapidly from film to digital photography. As manager of the corporate payroll department, I saw the employee population decline from over 20,000 employees in the mid-sixties to about 4,000 in the mid-nineties. After outsourcing the company payroll to ADP, I took advantage of a golden parachute opportunity, retired from Polaroid on a Friday and joined a small software company the following Monday, promising to give them two years of employment. It was certainly splendid to be able to "double-dip" during those two years leading up to total retirement.

Retirement

One year during February school vacation week, we visited some friends at their timeshare on the beach at Marco Island, Florida. It did not take long for us to also purchase a week; we then had a place to bring the kids during their winter break. The annual week gave us the opportunity to become familiar with the Naples, Florida, area. My wife retired at fifty-five and began a life of bridge, tennis, golf and shopping. After I finally retired, we looked around Naples and took a chance (which was very unlike the very conservative two of us) and bought into a new country club development. When we bought, the only thing completed was a beautiful golf course and a few model homes. We purchased a free standing golf villa on the tenth fairway and watched in amazement as the development of 731 units sold out in three short years and was turned over to the owners as a private club. It was a very fortunate purchase for us as the value of our investment has increased substantially. We both play tennis and golf as often as possible and enjoy the other activities of the club. Very surprisingly, my childhood friends Josh, Ray, Skip and I were all reunited in Naples and have resumed our friendships as if they had never been interrupted during those intervening fifty years.

We also maintain a small apartment in Swampscott, Massachusetts; we spend about seven months in Naples, five in Swampscott. Not a bad lifestyle for a kid from Dorchester. Such is life today, visiting kids, grandkids, friends and enjoying every day. We each have had a few health problems along the way, but feel so fortunate to have each other in reasonably good health and are thankful for every day we can get out of bed, put both our feet on the floor and go about our daily activities.

CHAPTER FOUR

The Poetry of Hank Heifetz

HANK HEIFETZ HAS PUBLISHED poetry, fiction, book-length literary translations from the languages of classical India and from Spanish, as well as many articles and reviews on the culture of India and on cinema. He has a PhD in the languages and culture of ancient India and has lived for long periods of time in India, Mexico and Italy. He has had shorter but deeply valued residences in Turkey and various countries of South America. He has also worked in documentary filmmaking and was the overall "creative director" of a three-year film project on Mexican history, politics and high and low culture, which was presented weekly on Mexican national television. He is currently writing "sort of" a novel as well as the initial stages for a series to be shown on American public television that will deal (if and when it is completed) with the rich, colorful and very complicated relationships over the last two centuries—politics, art and people to people—between the United States of Mexico and the United States of America. The poems included in "Dorchester Suite" were written in the sixties, seventies, and eighties.

DORCHESTER SUITE

1
Father, All Answers Fade Quick

geologic time, and billions
of years still to be drawn on
darkness by the galaxies
in which great fire your life's breath
sparkled
  and fed the blaze toward
                      end
father, in the cab of your
truck driving
    thirty-four years
till your head broke
in half at the foot of the iron
flight
  of stairs
              who are
              so dead
that your name has been cracked
in two and emptied of letters, and
talking to you
(who are so dead
you are two solemn
ritual months, the thirteenth and fourteenth in a calendar no
race keeps anymore)
is effort still but these many years easier
                    now
than when you were whole

and you rose four
o'clock in the morning
from your limbs'
        white warm rest
        cotton sheets and
        my mother
and buried your body inside brown
                sacking jacket
            cap and pants, clothes thick
                as planks
and went out,
        your forehead breaking the darkness
to work for us

father nothing

I wish your life had been
washed and lustrous
shining white
as you were when you had scraped the dirt
off and bathed and shaved
come home to us in the evening

I wish my life and your
life could have been the same high
    place

But you were held separate, always
you were in the power of the thing that hunts heads
crowded you into work that hurt your skull
dropped the iron awning bar only half a minute
              after you had leaned back into safety
cut your legs out from under you in a faint
    that laid your face inches from the iron radiator

and finally winning
in silence chanting over the pieces of you
at the iron stairs

father
once we were together one
instant in two bodies
becoming three
I hope
that moment of my mother will
   hang some memory of you on the atoms
                         of the air
till we are one again at the end of the world
which will be a flash of light
or of deep darkness
there is no difference in love

2
Where It Was

Nibble
at the trunk of the Tree of Good and Evil
located next to Whitman's Delicatessen
between Woolson Street and Hosmer Street in the lower
/Mattapan
part of Boston
hung with bras and prophylactics
leaves of hair
the same tree
the Kravitz twins tried to tear up the roots of
and made baseball bats out of some of the branches
swore at for a year
till their mother called them
and said to Herbert and Herman
'gnaw dead bark for the rest of your lives!'
after that they went I don't know where
throwing tincans at cats and dogs

This tree's
got a body that's notches
and caked sap in streamers
you and I and Lassie the Heroine Collie
can always get ourselves lost among these roots
but listen, this is the truth:
ONE MASTER IS NO BETTER THAN
/ANOTHER
and finding your way back home
(on your belly under wire
over 'Henry loves Helen 1947' dug into wood
and with your palms and your feet
bleeding)

79

couldn't wipe the sweat
off a hunter's hand in faraway Texas
holding a jackknife cutting open rabbits that
/tremble

corned beef and homesickness
without music
spoil on the ribbon
of chicken-soup cans
at the slope's foot
tree of choice
where my father dumped hot ashes
out of the furnace barrel
every winter Sunday
(now I know
snow and the melting of snow
is life)
you and I and everyone and all animals
may the remains of sandwiches
still be thrown out back of Whitman's Delicatessen
us grubbing through them whenever, if
we should happen to pass

3
In Memory of Arthur

I was born
only because my brother
died
screaming
his two months old body burning up
from within
and my mother peeling
off his skin
red dead pieces
of man tied the burns
tight to her nails
and eyes forever
passed them, later
to me, implanting
them, overprotecting
my touching, my breath
in her fear that
fire would come out of the sea for me

      all the naked bodies
                loving
   in darkness and light

women, men (the
      animals
   are a blur of hair and trees)
shut eyes, who have floated
    down through time
       what has come to be
       me
       these

sixty thousand
billion
cells!

the mouths swollen with each other
thigh bones
    biting in flow
all chance
  skin

 forever

nothing is destined
everything at the end of a
wilderness of strangled seeds
and solitudes
and babies dropped on the trail
and survivals and running
            flowerings
                    IS!

brother you who were never

given anything ripe but

                agony

thank you for my
life

4

If I decide to write from India
to my older only brother
who never taught me how to swim
how to ride a bike, any of the American
skills he would have had to be
the one to raise me up in because
my parents still were half in Europe
half in their new, never completely unalien land
and I was the classic favored younger son
shaped to glitter with literacy and scholarships
while you dropped from school
into the blue-collar morning
though you were tougher, just as bright, braver in your youth
but never my friend
while the mother small as a breeze
blew up a big wind at us
loving us and beating us
but sheltering me
and only battering you
now we move along different strips of the air
that surrounds and cradles the earth
against the freezing lack of touch
of Space
the same blood runs in us
as in the rest of humanity
after years of silence
something can be said
and along the avenue of our childhood
　　　　they've long ago boarded up the stores

5

That diner way out lonely
under the tracks, in the middle of tracks
in Charlestown Boston by the docks
where I went with Joe Esposito
cutting out on his wife to hunt women
with me, his young friend from the factory
is my image of the edge of existence
with the runaway boys the gay owner has
taken in with him for some days hanging around
the entrance and a few wasted girls
and the small-time, poor hoods
sitting around with their cups of coffee
and the factory girls who sweat all day
looking for someone with at least a little money
to come by and want them
where Joe Esposito never paid
except with a glance at the owner for any of our
hamburgers or cokes
because down here among the lost Joe was a king
being dark Neapolitan handsome, only men with money
were worth more
and we took the two sisters from there
to the apartment they shared with a third,
and in bed mine was ugly and faded and wouldn't
open her legs
so after a while I left her and waiting for Joe
I met the other sister,
the youngest, as beautiful as a renaissance madonna
who was waiting with uneasy hope
for the arrival of some man
who was late and in the hour or two
we talked we fell in love

and would have held to each other all night long
but her friend, a hood
in his thirties, with a big white hat
finally arrived and went to her room and her bed
and she left me with a long look
and I never saw her dark brown eyes
again except in paintings

6
For Dorchester

That's how the old neighborhood vanished
in an ocean of heroin
sweeping over the leftover
teen-age children of those Jews with
        not enough money to leave
kids flung against the walls
police clubs jabbing
and the long years of the children
        drying out in drug programs
and the scattered dead
and then the stores of my childhood
desires changed one after another
into something utterly not me

Chapter Five

Paul Rosenthal

M Y PARENTS WERE EDWARD and Sarah Rosenfield Rosenthal. My mother grew up in Chelsea, Massachusetts, and moved to Ziegler Street near Dudley Street station in Roxbury; my father grew up in Malden, Massachusetts. They met at Revere Beach in 1931—she was there with a date and he was with friends. Somehow he ended up filing her nails on their first meeting and they were married a few years later.

On March 10, 1935, I entered the world near Harvard Yard at the Mount Auburn Hospital in Cambridge. I was a second generation Bostonian. The family lore is that my parents got a dog a few days before I was born and named the dog Peter, the name they had been planning on using for me. I was then named Paul. My brother David was born in 1938 and my sister Jane in 1946. My family moved in 1939 to 28 Supple Road, a two family house in a middle-class Jewish neighborhood in Dorchester. My Aunt Betty, my mom's sister, lived downstairs and my older cousins served as built-in babysitters.

Due to some bureaucratic description of birthdays that interpreted me as too young for kindergarten one year and too old the following year, I skipped kindergarten. My wife says I missed the best year of school. My parents chose the school my brother and I went to so we would have a better chance of getting into Boston Latin. The William Lloyd Garrison School in Dorchester was about three-quarters of a mile from home. The only teacher I remember at the school was the headmistress, Miss Gallagher; she was tough. Although my children can't believe our teachers would hit us, Miss Gallagher gave my brother the "rat hand" for throwing snowballs.

It was in primary school that my brother and I joined AZA (Aleph Tzadik Aleph, the American Zionist Association), an organization for young Jewish boys. Our meetings were held at the Hecht House in Dorchester. We collected newspapers, cans and whatever else our young civic-minded selves deemed was necessary for the war effort.

In the late 1930s and early 1940s my father ran a summer day camp in Nantasket Beach on the south shore of Boston. I was too young to attend but I enjoyed the beach and playing stick ball on the street while my brother watched from my mother's arms.

My dad was a biology teacher at Girls' High School in Boston and often drove my brother, my friends and me to school. Since my father also had a second job, in the family laundry business in Dorchester, we would usually walk home. As I grew older my friends and I were faced with local non-Jewish boys who tried to shove us, take our money, and chase us when we walked home from school. I remember being surrounded by twenty hostile boys and our Hebrew School teacher chasing them away. This was a time of Jewish families in Dorchester moving to the suburbs. This was also the beginning of my track career in short-distance running and hurdling puddles. My family moved to Newton, where my sister started in the Newton schools, one of the best systems in the country.

In the summer of 1941 my father, aka Pop, went to Camp Alton in Wolfeboro, New Hampshire, to work as a camp counselor. The director, Philip Marson, an English teacher at Boston Latin was so impressed with Pop that he invited my mom, my brother and me to spend a week vacationing at camp. All three of us were very excited. This was the beginning of a long relationship with the Marsons, the Rosenthals and Lake Winnipesaukee. David and I went as campers the next year. After years of being campers and counselors, David and I built a house on Lake Winnipesaukee in 1985. Our families enjoyed the house long after the camp was closed, and my wife and I recently sold our share in the house to David and Judy. I had a superb sixty-five-year relationship with Wolfeboro and Lake Winnipesaukee.

Early in our track careers, David and I realized that since the camp laundry was done by our family in Boston, there were trucks going between Boston and Wolfeboro all summer. We convinced Mr. Fitzgerald, our fantastic Latin School track coach, to allow the hurdles to be shipped to camp, and convinced our family to do the shipping. We trained all year and then all summer. I became state champion in the high hurdles in my senior year of high school, and in his senior year David was the New England low hurdles champion and one of the best runners and hurdlers out of Boston Latin.

Camp for me was like a family reunion. For years, my dad was assistant director of the camp and my mother was in charge of the well-being of many campers and the canteen. At camp, David and I usually gave our parents a "hello," a friendly wave, and a very quick goodbye. On visiting days we would spend more time with our friends' parents than our own. I had so many friends and relatives who attended: Norton Levy, Jay Rosenfield, Peter Ross, Ralph Aserkoff, Peter Hoffman, Carl and Michael Roberts, Lenny Wollins, Carl Roberts, David Rosenthal (brother), Laura Hrasky (niece), Keith Hrasky (nephew), Jim Rosenthal (son), Jimmy, Michael and Allen Tofias, Sugar, Richie and Roy Robinson, Joe Sheffer, Steve Mirsky, Michael and Marty

Doctoroff, Victor Freedman, Ed Ellis, Larry Halperin, Carl and Barry Rosenthal and many others. My only disappointment associated with Camp Alton came in the form of my son, Jimmy, telling my wife and me that he did not want to go back for a third summer. He wanted to stay home and play competitive tennis. We relented and his tennis career took off.

Part of what I loved about camp was that the activities held my interest for different reasons when I was at different ages. I remember being scared by the snipe hunt as a camper (and loving it) and scaring the campers as a counselor (and loving it). As campers, we were told that snipes went after your eyes and so we needed to stand under a tree with our eyes closed or blindfolded. We were told the snipe fell into a laundry bag and one of the counselors would shake the bag so we would think we had caught one. We would deliver the bag to a designated building and the bag would return covered with blood (or at least ketchup). The next morning we drank snipe juice with breakfast. The snipe hunts ended before my son went to camp because the campers were complaining to their parents that it was too scary. Capture the Flag also held my interest for all my years there; flags of different values were based on the camper's age and there was a jail for campers who were captured before they could take a flag back to their side. But the best part was the all-camp rush: when the senior counselors decided to send over all their rushers at the same time.

In my first year at Harvard (1952-53) I roomed with Irving Zola, who also prepared at Latin School. He was one of the brightest students I met at Harvard; Irv had contracted polio as a teenager and died when he was only fifty-nine. My other roommate was Chuck Edison from St. Louis, Missouri. I don't get to see Chuck that much but enjoy catching up with him at reunions. I roomed with Irving and Chuck for one year. In my sophomore year (1953-54) I had three roommates: Arthur Bloom (BLS), George Wolkon (BLS), and Norman Bruck

(Weequaic High School) from Newark, New Jersey. The four of us were assigned to Leverett House, but because of over-crowding we roomed during sophomore year at Claverly Hall. In my junior and senior years George and I roomed together at Leverett House. It was a wonderful time in our lives and I thank my roommates for being a part of it.

Arthur has become a long-distance friend. For the years he was in New York and we were in Boston we brought our families together. In October 2003, Shae and I and six other classmates with spouses joined Arthur and Deborah at their home in Saint-Germain-En-Laye, just outside of Paris. The highlight of the trip was a visit to the Bloom's charming house in Normandy. We took a walk on Normandy Beach, visited the Omaha Beach cemetery, walked on Deauville Beach, which had movie stars' names on lockers, went to a great spa, and stayed at an inn at the small fishing village in Honfleur. Deborah served a wonderful meal and afterwards Arthur ran an AZA meeting similar to the ones we had at the Hecht House.

Archie has done a great job in organizing the AZA group and he deserves a round of applause. George Wolkon lives in Los Angeles and we get together at reunions. (*Ed. Note:* Barbara Wolkon died in 2008.) I met Norman Bruck in my first year, when both of us went out for the Harvard track team. Norm was a great runner and since I ran and hurdled in high school and camp I concentrated on the hurdles. Unfortunately, Norm, who became a lawyer, died just short of his thirty-ninth birthday from a brain tumor.

I started off as an engineering major and ended with a liberal arts degree. I chose engineering because I was good in math but found out very quickly that being a good math student had no relationship to engineering. Fifty-one years later I am still getting information from the engineering school at Harvard.

I ran track for a few years and then concentrated on graduating. Although getting my diploma was one of the happiest days of my young life, I did not know what I wanted to do next. I did what so many of my generation did when faced with uncertainty: I enlisted in the army. I served two years at Fort Dix, New Jersey, as a clerk typist. My next-door roommate was Rosey Grier, a defensive lineman for the New York Giants.

When finishing my army commitment I considered joining my uncles' laundry business. I had worked summers there in the diaper department. I was good at it and it was familiar. My uncles convinced me to take a series of exams to see what I was fitted for. To no great surprise the test confirmed my expertise in typing, saying "Yes, sir" and saluting. Luckily, the test also showed I had expertise in finance and accounting. My parents were very happy when I decided that I would not go to work in the family business but would further my education.

I enrolled at Bentley College, an accounting school in Boston. After school and during the summer I worked at the laundry. After two years at Bentley I was hired by Peat, Marwick, Mitchell (PMM) one of the "big eight" accounting firms. On the request of Jewish clients, the firm was beginning to hire Jewish accountants. This was my very first full-time job and I was thrilled. I started as a junior accountant and within two years I was the senior accountant on the Gillette account.

It was at this point that I met the love of my life. Good friends of my parents had a daughter I had known my whole life. The daughter's college roommate at Lesley College in Cambridge, Massachusetts, was Shae Shepatin. I had never met anyone as lovely and nice as Shae. She was smart, pretty, outgoing, and I was determined to make her Mrs. Paul Rosenthal. Shae and I were married on June 26, 1960, shortly after she graduated college. We might have chosen to get married sooner but her father was determined to have his last name on her college diploma!

We moved to 58 Duff Street in Watertown, paid $105 per month for our garden apartment, and felt like we were in the penthouse suite. Mike and Jackie Klein were our neighbors. As most of our neighbors were either graduate students or medical residents, I was one of the few that kept regular business hours. Debbie, our first child, was born on April 4, 1961, and we were ecstatic. On November 5, 1963, son Jimmy was born. We were excited that we now had a girl and a boy.

During my years at Peat, Marwick, Mitchell & Co., I audited a variety of clients that included retailers, healthcare providers, the Boston Museum of Fine Arts, electronics companies, and service companies. My job included reconciling inventories, analyzing accounts, reconciling bank accounts, discussing problems with senior employees, and assessing all other accounting problems. My experience gave me great training and connections for future jobs. At that time I didn't realize how important either the training and connections were or how many jobs were in my future.

From 1959 until my retirement, forty-six years later, I had ten jobs for an average of 4.5 years per job. I did not have a master plan. As I tried to enhance my education and self-audit my situation, I found myself with both opportunities and disasters. With each job, I became better at assessing my role. If the job was not for me, I made a change as soon as possible. Luckily, my resume of Boston Latin, Harvard, and the track team seemed to impress potential employers so there was always another job on the horizon.

In 1964 I became an internal auditor at General Time, a clock maker, and we moved to Riverdale, New York. Commuting into the city I could read *The New York Times* from beginning to end. My auditing job took me to places like Skokie, Illinois, and York, Pennsylvania. My job wasn't as interesting as I had hoped and then I got a call to come back to Boston to work for a company that I had audited while at PMM.

I was offered the job as controller for Spencer Kennedy, an electronic equipment manufacturer. We bought a house in the

Chestnut Hill part of Newton, where we resided for twenty-eight years. Mike Klein served as the lawyer in the purchase of our house. Spencer Kennedy was a pioneer in the cable industry but it turned out that their new system had a few flaws. When lighting struck, the entire system went down. Luckily, they made solid standard electronic equipment.

Our third child, Margi, was born on March 25, 1967. She claims we bought the four-bedroom house in Chestnut Hill because we were planning on a family of five.

I have always had a penchant for numbers: my wife often recalls an early date when I taught her how to play cribbage with car license plates. Accounting was my vocation and I am always putting numbers together to find patterns. I could list the myriad ways why five is my lucky number but suffice it to say that until my children got married, we were a family of five; we spent twenty-eight years at 5 Harwich Road in Newton; and now we live at 5 Alfred Lane in Stamford, Connecticut.

Next, I went to work for a national consulting firm, Coopers Lybrand. At Lybrand I learned more about accounting but above all I was taught how to dissect a company and uncover accounting problems, which proved to be extremely helpful in later years.

In 1972 I had three different jobs. In my first (and next to last) day at Honey Farms, a small grocery chain, I noticed that the phones never stopped ringing. It turned out to be creditors looking for their money.

One day, when I was home with the children between jobs, my mother dropped in and asked what I was doing at home. I was looking for work. It was not very pleasant.

I began my thirty-two years as controller and CFO in the distribution industry at Parts Distributor (1972-76), a distributor of auto parts, and Northeastern Wallpaper (1977-85), a distributor of wallpaper. Both companies were privately owned and sales were $25 to $50 million. My twelve years at these two companies was excellent training for the twenty years I would spend at D.F. Munroe.

A good friend from a previous job, John Gallagher, provided computer services to D.F. Munroe, and introduced me to the owners. At this time D.F. Munroe was a $20 million distributor of fine paper, with four locations in the New England area. John Gallagher was very helpful in the transition, and in no time I was making changes. With twelve years of working in two different distribution companies, I was able to combine that experience with that of D.F. Munroe and pick the best of the three companies. I helped the company grow another $10 to $15 million into a practically new and very smooth running company. This also helped later when we combined D.F. Munroe into Lindenmeyr. Soon Central National Gottesman (CNG), a privately owned company, approached us to consider purchase.

One complication of the deal was that CNG already owned a paper distributor and already had a controller for their paper division. For one year there were two controllers. I frequently traveled to CNG headquarters in Purchase, New York. In 1992 I was there so often I rented an apartment in nearby White Plains. If I stayed through the weekend, Shae would take the train down and sometimes she'd stay longer. You could say the apartment was a "dump."

In 1993, Shae and I realized the boarding-room situation was not a long-term solution. We rented an apartment in Old Greenwich, Connecticut, and nine months later bought a condo in a gated community in Stamford, Connecticut. We had moved twenty minutes from corporate headquarters and remain in that house today.

The anticipation of the move was difficult and exciting—we had lived in our Newton home for twenty-eight years, I was Boston-born and bred, and Shae had been there for almost all of her adult life. We were fortunate that our children were independent and did not have to be relocated. Debbie graduated from the University of Massachusetts in 1983, received her MBA from Babson College in 1991 and at that time was working for Teradyne in Boston. Jimmy had graduated from Harvard in 1985 and was working at Booz, Allen & Hamilton in New York, and Margi had graduated from Harvard in 1989 and was a Yale medical student. We were also fortunate in that it seemed everyone we knew had a gracious friend in either Fairfield or Westchester county.

And to be clear, I remain a Bostonian in my heart: I was beside myself with joy when the Red Sox won the World Series; I went to the Patriots Super Bowl in Jacksonville with my son; and whenever the Boston Symphony is in New York, Shae and I go to Carnegie Hall.

The twenty years at Lindenmeyr Munroe gave me the opportunity to apply the knowledge and training I had gained in my vast experience. At first, there was no change in the way we and (CNG) ran our business. It took a little time to combine the two companies. The smooth turnover of the two companies into one company impressed top management. The controller of Lindenmeyr saw the handwriting on the wall and realized that I was going to be in charge. He stayed on for a while and eventually I took over the seven branches. I now had to put my organization in place. I made David Jones (yes, that's his name) assistant controller of Lindenmeyr Munroe and he transferred to the Purchase office. In no time we were well organized and we started to buy branches in Richmond, Virginia, and Chicago, Illinois. Our sales increased at a fast pace and we were ahead of forecast.

On January 1, 2005, just short of my seventy-first birthday, I retired from the workforce. I had had a rewarding forty-five years. Although there were many reasons for this success, the number-one reason was my wife, the cheerleader. With all the ups and downs, she was always there to support me.

I now have been retired for one and a half years. During the first few months I was content catching up on little tasks and maintaining my hobbies and commitments. I remain treasurer of both the Everett Credit Union in Everett, Massachusetts, and our homeowners association. I collect first day of issue stamps and have some from the 1920s.

As time went by the tasks started to disappear and I became bored. I read novels, followed sports, went to the movies and played more tennis, golf and bridge. I needed more. So I did what so many of my generation used to do but have not done in years. I joined two new organizations. I joined SMASH (Senior Men's Association of Stamford), a weekly men's group where we have had speakers on the Sikh religion, robotic surgery, the Holocaust and the Jewish Community Endowment Foundation.

I also joined SCORE (Senior Counselors Organization for Retired Executives). SCORE provides free professional guidance to existing and emerging small businesses. I have assisted SCORE clients that make rugs, run private eating clubs, make gourmet sauces, are professional speakers, organize local trash collecting, distribute organic hair- and body-care products, as well as the local food bank. I find it rewarding to use the part of my brain that stores forty-six years of accounting knowledge and I enjoy the thanks I receive from the clients. I am, by the way, amazed that a small jar of sauce can be valued at $8 in a gourmet market. In October 2007 I became treasurer of the Fairfield County SCORE chapter and treasurer of the Fairfield County Food Bank.

In August 2007 I volunteered at the Pilot Pen Tennis Tournament in New Haven, Connecticut, where I ushered, played miniature tennis with the young ones, and took tickets. One day I worked at court level watching a semi-final match for women. I couldn't believe how hard they hit.

I feel fortunate to have such a rich life. Everything has gone well except for a single devastating tragedy that occurred in our daughter Margi's life. Her husband, Amal, was a pediatric critical care physician at University of North Carolina, and they were living in Chapel Hill. Driving home from their vacation, Amal and his brother were in the front car while Margi, their two children and her sister-in-law were behind them. A tire blew on Amal's car and the car rolled over. Amal died instantly and his brother sustained major injuries.

I am also fortunate to have so many old friends from Boston and new friends in and around Stamford. Our friends in Boston usually stop by for a bite or sleepover on their way to New York City.

Our children surround us, as they live in Princeton, New York City and New Haven. Debbie lives in Princeton, New Jersey, and has been married fourteen years to Jason Bronfeld. Debbie is an executive director for a non-profit, Dress For Success. Jason is an executive director of pharmaceutical development information at Bristol Myers Squibb. They have two boys, Maxwell and Harrison, in third and sixth grade. Jimmy has been married to Helene Mirkis for twenty years. They have twin daughters, Samantha and Zoe, in ninth grade at the Trinity School in New York City. The girls were B'not Mitzvah last spring, and Shae and I were beside ourselves with pride. Helene, when she is not taking care of the twins, and Jimmy are starting a business designing and selling greeting cards based on her photography and wit. Jimmy is now chief executive of Kaplan Professionals (the education company that is a division of the Washington Post). Kaplan Professionals trains students to obtain and maintain professional licenses in the fields of financial services, accounting, real estate and information technology. Margi was married to Amal Murarka in 1999. They have two daughters, Elina and Maya, going into kindergarden and second grade. Amal died in 2003. Margi is now a pediatrician at Yale and lives with her partner, Richard Bell, also a young widower and also a doctor, originally from the Boston area. He is finishing his residency in psychiatry at the University of Connecticut in Farmington, Connecticut. This coming year Richard will have a fellowship in psychiatry at Yale. He and his twin eleven-year-old daughters, Hannah and Lucy, moved in with Margi's family, and you can imagine what the house is like.

Hopefully, Shae and I will be doing a lot of traveling. In November 2007 we spent two weeks in Israel and Jordan. I also spent a full day (as a patient) at the hospital in Tiberis, Israel.

I have enjoyed writing this memoir and am looking forward to reading all the others. It has been an interesting, soul searching project. Some of the facts I wrote about had been a little vague in my mind but as has been true throughout my life, I had siblings, cousins, friends and especially my wife to help me with the details.

I am not the classmate I was in 1952, as I have since had orthoscopic surgery on my knee, had a pacemaker implanted, have hearing aids and a retainer and am currently having radiation for prostate cancer. All thanks to modern medicine. Nonetheless, despite it all, I feel good!

Chapter Six

Jerry Davidow

GROWING UP IN ROXBURY during the 1940s, I had a hankering to be someplace else, even though my part of Roxbury was a pretty nice place then. My family lived in a spacious and attractive single-family house at the bottom of Elm Hill Avenue, near Warren Street and only a few blocks from Blue Hill Avenue. The trolleys went by just a few steps away, there was a drugstore on the corner and a small grocery store, a bakery selling "bulkies" (or rolls) for two cents each, a shoemaker and a barber shop. My favorite was the drugstore, which had a fancy marble soda fountain and where I went almost every day to buy an ice cream cone for five cents.

Across the street from my house was the African Methodist Episcopalian Church, which buzzed with beautifully dressed parishioners every Sunday morning. Next to the church was the Menorah Hebrew School, but my family patronized the fancier Mishkan Tefila Temple, a half-dozen blocks away at the top of Elm Hill Avenue, at the corner of Seaver Street. I hated Mishkan Tefila, because I was required to go its Hebrew School every weekday afternoon and every Sunday morning. I would rather have spent my time playing in the streets, or maybe even doing my Latin School homework, which usually got only short shrift. I probably have never recovered from the antipathy to organized religion that going to Hebrew school engendered in me.

Elm Hill Avenue was graced with beautiful, old elm trees, befitting the street's name, but the 1938 hurricane had damaged some of them, and the scourge of Dutch elm disease was advancing rapidly. Nevertheless, the street had a somewhat worn beauty. We lived next door to Frederick Mansfield, who was the last "Yankee" mayor of Boston in the 1930s. His house was separated from mine by a generous rose garden. Elm Hill Avenue was just steep enough to make for thrilling sled rides after a winter storm and for terrifying roller-skating in the spring and fall. Automobile traffic was not a problem, because few people drove cars then, given the shortages of gasoline and tires brought on by the Second World War. Crime was not a problem either, because most of the young hoodlums had been sent off to serve in the army.

My father was a physician and had his office and waiting room in the front of our house, so there were always people coming and going. I had to be quiet when there were patients waiting to see my father. My favorite place was the big basement, where my older brother had set up a photography darkroom, and where there was a ping-pong table and a Victrola, and a corner just next to the furnace where I set up my chemistry laboratory. My Uncle Joe had given me a chemistry set complete with Bunsen burner and test tubes, and I was fascinated by its possibilities. I spent hours fiddling with chemistry compounds, mostly trying to make gunpowder. One day I succeeded in creating a sufficiently powerful explosion so that my father, a pretty stern man, shut down the laboratory for good. So ended my budding career as a research scientist.

JERRY DAVIDOW

The First Stirrings

Even though gasoline was pretty hard to obtain for most folks, as a physician making house calls, my father had a regular supply for his automobile. I should mention that in those days my father charged two dollars for office visits and three dollars for house calls, so he was always willing to make house calls, because the extra money came in handy. Nobody had medical insurance in those days, and my father was not always paid in cash, but everyone seemed to pay him whatever they could. By the standards of the day, we lived luxuriously.

Almost every Sunday, the family climbed into the Dodge and we drove to a pretty fancy restaurant in Hingham or Whitman or Framingham to have dinner. Occasionally we drove into Boston's Chinatown for dinner, which usually consisted of egg foo young and Chicago chow mein. This was exotic stuff. In the summer, after school closed, we drove out to our "country" home at Nantasket Beach, my mother and I staying there until Labor Day, while my father commuted each weekend. This routine was interrupted for a couple of years during the war, when the house was rented out to defense workers at the Fore River shipyards.

My father had a good friend who was a physician living in Brockton. He had moved there after getting in trouble in Boston for performing a mysterious "illegal operation." We would drive to Brockton occasionally to see the kindly abortionist, or to Sharon to visit another friend's gentleman farm, or to New Bedford, where we had some relatives. After the war ended, we drove occasionally to Albany to visit my mother's older brother or to New York City to visit my father's brother and his sister. All in all, my travel experiences were modest.

The big travel event happened in 1946, when my oldest brother returned from the army, after serving in the Battle of the Bulge in Europe and the occupation army in Japan. In celebration of the event, we made a road trip through New York State, visiting Ithaca, where my father had gone to college at Cornell, to Cooperstown at my insistence to see the Baseball Hall of Fame, to the Thousand Islands, then to Buffalo to visit my brother's army buddy, then to Montreal and on to Quebec City. On the highway to Quebec City, we passed a convoy of open cars carrying Field Marshal Montgomery, the hero of El Alamein. We went nuts, cheering and waving at him! The generals who had fought World War II were everyone's heroes in those days.

We returned to Boston, traveling through New Hampshire, stopping for dinner one day at a roadside diner in White River Junction. There was a really cute young waitress serving us, who I was certain was making eyes at me, and I fell in love. I was eleven years old. Of course, I never saw her again and my infatuation faded after a few years, but I have never forgotten her. I wonder if she still thinks about me.

I attended the William Lloyd Garrison Elementary School, skipping a grade in the "rapid advancement" program, then went on to the Boston Latin School to complete my secondary education. I wasn't a particularly distinguished scholar at Boston Latin School, but I did excel in the extracurricular stuff, becoming editor in chief of the school's literary magazine, vice president of the debating club and also editor in chief of the yearbook. These accomplishments secured a position for me in the large group from Boston Latin School who entered Harvard, from which I graduated in 1956 with an honors degree in economics.

Wow! An Airplane

The first time I ever set foot on an airplane was on June 18, 1956, the day after I got married, at age twenty. There were other firsts that week, but that's not part of this story. My new wife and I were on our way to our honeymoon in Bermuda, with reservations for two weeks at the Castle Harbour Hotel. I have absolutely no recollection of how we paid for this trip, which must have cost a pretty penny, but wedding gifts must have covered it. We might have wanted to stay at the fancier Elbow Beach Hotel in Bermuda, but we were advised that they did not welcome Jews. The plane trip was uneventful, but we were happy to discover that another couple whom we knew had been married the same day and were traveling to the same destination.

The Castle Harbour Hotel was perfectly fine, but a tad stiff. So was the other couple that we had encountered on the plane, so we spent little time with them. I remember asking a waiter one day if he would bring me some mustard, and he asked whether I preferred French or English mustard. I hadn't a clue, but I took a stab at asking for French mustard and I was rewarded by the old familiar standby of yellow mustard. After a week at the Castle Harbour Hotel, during most of which it rained, Barbara and I had enough of Bermuda, with a week yet to go. Let me pause here to say that the Barbara of this early narrative is not the same Barbara of the later years. Both my first and hopefully last wife are named Barbara, but they are two very different people.

At this point in the narrative, Barbara and I met another honeymooning couple, who had been pretty adventurous and had explored some of the back streets in Hamilton. We joined them one night at a dark and a little menacing music club well off the tourist path, where we were just about the only white people. The music was Jamaican reggae, which I had never heard before. It blew my mind. The marriage didn't last, but the attraction to unusual music forms is with me still.

The Quiet Years

After graduating from Harvard College, I moved on to the Harvard Business School, graduating from that august institution in 1958. The next ten years offered little opportunity for travel. I had taken a position with Macy's New York after finishing school, had two kids, bought a house in the New York suburbs and put my nose to the grindstone. Money was usually tight. We had one nice vacation trip to Puerto Rico, where I made a good score at the blackjack table; lots of trips back to Boston to visit family; and an occasional business trip to such exotic locales as New Haven.

At Macy's, I got deeply involved in putting on the famous Thanksgiving Day parade, becoming one of the grand marshals who led the parade down Broadway. This was fun, but otherwise my career at Macy's languished. I finally realized that Macy's wasn't meant for me (and vice versa), so I left after seven years and worked as a product manager for a couple of years at a toiletries manufacturer. A change in management convinced me that it was time for another job change, so I went to work at a small advertising agency, where I stayed for the next twenty years. By 1968, I was earning a little more money and got the urge to travel.

A friend of mine had just sold off his childhood comic book collection for enough money to fund a family trip out West to visit the national parks, and I was jealous of his good fortune. I decided that we should take a similar trip and priced out an itinerary to take us to Yellowstone, the Grand Canyon and a few other spots. I was a bit stunned at what this would cost, and at one point said that we could probably all go to Europe for less. That did it. We booked a package trip for the four of us on Air India, to spend one week in Paris and a second week in London, hotels included. I extracted a promise from the kids that they wouldn't fuss over the strange foreign food.

Paris!

We landed at Orly Airport and headed to the Left Bank, with our vouchers in hand for accommodations at the crumbling Dagmar Hotel. Madame, the proprietress, showed Barbara and me to our room, which was more than shabby but tolerable. Then we went to see the kids' room, which was on a different floor at the end of a really scary long hallway. I could see the panic in Amy and Judy's eyes. They were only eleven and nine years old and they didn't want to be separated from their parents in a strange city, in a musty old hotel where everyone talked funny.

I protested vigorously to Madame, announcing in my primitive French that these rooms were simply not acceptable. Madame put up a spirited resistance, but finally said that there was only one other option, if we would agree to all four of us sharing the same room. We went to look at the room, which was amazing! It must have once been the ballroom of the Dagmar Hotel in better days, because it was ornately decorated in a style reminiscent of Miss Havisham's parlor in *Great Expectations*. The room went on for thirty or so feet, went up for fifteen feet, and was just the thing for us. We were delighted.

We were also starving. We hadn't had anything to eat except the strange curries on Air India, so we set off in search of sustenance. It was mid-afternoon and the restaurants were all closed, but we found an establishment that agreed to serve the savage Americains at this odd hour. We all ordered simple omelets. They were made from the freshest eggs, rich in cream and butter, served with fresh baguettes, and were the best thing that any of us had ever eaten. So much for the kids resisting foreign food. Within a day they were happily tucking into their Supremes de Vollaille Cordon Bleu and comparing notes on each day's mousse au chocolat. Things have never been the same since.

Barbara had family in Paris, who had gotten lost there on the way from Poland to the goldeneh medina back in the 1920s, had survived World War II in good shape by traveling to Spain, and had prospered in France as manufacturers of handbags. We had met the whole mishpocheh in New York when they had come to the United States after visiting the Montreal World's Fair. When we got settled in the Hotel Dagmar, the family found us and invited us to dinner at their home—not an invitation to be taken lightly in Paris.

We arrived at their address in the Marais neighborhood of Paris and discovered that it was an ancient factory and warehouse. This was long before Le Marais became the chic neighborhood that it is today. We found the creaky old elevator and went slowly up to the top floor of the factory, where we unloaded into a magnificent apartment that seemed to go on forever. It was beautifully furnished with fine old furniture and occupied by perhaps twenty cousins and cousins of cousins, who had all gathered to greet us. They spoke no English, we spoke almost no French, some of us spoke a bit of Yiddish, but not me. We all got along beautifully.

We settled into the living room for cocktails, featuring the biggest bottle of Scotch whisky that I had ever seen. The French are used to opening a bottle of wine and finishing it, so it seemed logical to them that we would finish the bottle of Scotch before settling down to dinner. By the time we sat down for dinner, we were all looped. Even the children seemed a bit tipsy, maybe from the fumes. Dinner was a great success, and by the end of the evening they were speaking a bit of English, I had remembered my Latin School French, and Barbara had recaptured her Bobbeh's Yiddish. We all kissed and hugged our new relatives and went rolling happily out the door at midnight. The rest of our week in Paris was equally wonderful.

London!

Now it was on to Holland Park in London, with our vouchers in hand allowing us to stay in a once-grand Georgian mansion, now a hotel that had fallen on hard times. We were shown to our rooms, which were perfectly adequate, but I decided that it wouldn't hurt to put on the same show that had worked so well at the Hotel Dagmar. I told the proper English proprietor that the rooms simply would not do. He protested that he had nothing else to show us, except that there was a basement dormitory room that was presently unoccupied. If the four of us would stay in one room, we could have the entire dormitory to ourselves. We were shown to the dormitory, which had a dozen single beds, a huge bathroom with several shower stalls and a number of sinks, and a big laundry room. We couldn't have been happier if we were lodged in the grandest five-star hotel.

After two glorious weeks, it was back to the real world in New York. The trip was a great experience and I had spent less than $1,500 for the whole thing, including hotels, souvenirs, meals and airfares. God bless Air India!

The Holy Land

Daughter Amy spent the summer of 1973 in a kibbutz in Israel picking peaches, with a week off from slave labor to tour the country. Wife and I, with mother-in-law in tow, decided to visit Amy during her travel break in Israel. The organization in charge of Amy's kibbutz program was disinclined to share her itinerary with us, citing security grounds, but we took our chances that we would be able to find her. After all, it's a very small country. We arrived in Tel Aviv and discovered that Amy was at the Golan Heights. We traveled to the Golan Heights and found out that Amy was now in the Negev. We hot-tailed it to the Negev and Amy had moved on to Haifa. We gave up trying to catch up with her, spoke to her on the telephone and promised that we would see her back in New York in a couple of weeks. Mirabile dictu, as we were nosing around the central square in Bethlehem, a tour bus unloaded and there was Amy!

Many hugs later, we parted from daughter Amy and traveled on to Rome for a week's visit before returning to New York.

Rome was hot as blazes and we struggled mightily to see all the usual tourist sights. As we straggled out of the Vatican Library one day, impressed as all get-out with the marvels of the Catholic Church, we were hungry, dying of thirst and deeply sympathizing with the ancient Jews who had been tossed to the lions in the nearby Colosseum. Stationed in front of us on the outskirts of the Vatican was a fruit vendor peddling peaches from his cart. Maybe the best peaches that I have ever eaten!

More of Europe

On one occasion, I had to travel to Denmark on business for a Monday meeting, and decided to get there a few days early to see the sights and enjoy Copenhagen over the weekend. I had introductions to some business associates there, who, I was assured, would take me in hand and make me feel at home. When I sought them out, they were cordial but their hospitality was limited to handing me a list of restaurants that might be of interest. Discouraged, I wandered alone into Tivoli Gardens and was immediately overwhelmed by the beauty and charm of the place. It's a cross between Central Park in New York City and Lincoln Center, with a little bit of Disneyland thrown in for good measure. I met a wonderful young woman as I strolled around Tivoli Gardens, who showed me the sights of Copenhagen and kept me company through the weekend. At one point, I wandered into a jazz club and was immediately adopted by a gaggle of young Danes, who insisted that I join their party. By the end of the evening I had accumulated more friends in

Denmark than I had back in the U.S.A. It was magical.

Stanley, the chairman of my advertising agency, called me while I was in Copenhagen and asked me to stop in London to pick up his humidor of Cuban cigars and bring them back to New York City. When I asked how I was to smuggle these contraband cigars into the country, he told me not to worry. I figured that if I was going to spend a few years in prison for smuggling, I might as well go all the way, so I stopped at a bakery in Copenhagen and filled a suitcase with the fabulous Danish pastry, which the Danes perversely call Vienna Bread. I arrived at Kennedy Airport with a suitcase full of cigars, another suitcase full of pastry and a small parcel of my clothing and toiletries. In minutes, I was whisked through customs by a friendly inspector and found my car and driver to take me home. Not for the first time, I marveled at Stanley's insidious ways. The family gorged on pastry that night.

The Seventies

The rest of the seventies were kind of complicated for me. Nixon resigned the presidency, I got divorced, then I remarried, then quickly divorced again. As my personal life plummeted downward, my career in advertising seemed to prosper. This required me to do a great deal of travel, mostly in the United States, and mostly to business destinations. I've been all over the United States, but if the truth be known, most airports look a lot alike, most Marriott Hotels are pretty much the same, and, with few exceptions, the only way I knew where I was traveling was by checking my airline tickets. The one saving grace is that my company required—not permitted, required!—that all of its employees travel first class and stay in luxury hotels, so travel was generally very pleasant. I especially liked Chicago, San Francisco, New Orleans and Beverly Hills (but you can keep the rest of Los Angeles.)

In Pittsburgh I came down with a stunning case of the mumps and had to return home tout de suite. My family physician took one look at me and asked me to leave by the side door, so as not to frighten the other patients. Detroit wasn't dull either, but it was not because of the charms of the city. I had nothing to do one night, and Detroit was not the kind of city where one wandered around aimlessly, so I decided to see the movie Z, which was playing at a theater nearby. There were only a few of us in the theater, and as the movie came to its riveting conclusion, wisps of smoke started to curl around the screen. No one moved. Finally, at the most exciting part of the finale, the projector was turned off to our disappointment, we heard the sirens of fire engines in the distance, and a theater employee asked us to please exit the auditorium immediately. We then stood on the sidewalk across the street and watched the theater burn to the ground.

My second marriage was short lived, and I nearly became short lived myself, as I awoke one night to find my bride standing over me with a menacing knife. I decided that things weren't working out in the marriage, and departed to a hotel room, not to return. But we had a couple of interesting trips before things got totally out of control.

On one such trip we traveled to Puerto Vallarta, on the west coast of Mexico. Puerto Vallarta is now a big city, bustling with condo developments and thronged with gringos, but then it was little more than a remote fishing village, having been discovered a couple of years earlier by Richard Burton and Elizabeth Taylor while making *The Night of the Iguana*. We loved Puerto Vallarta, had a wonderful casita right on the beach, and were serenaded by mariachi bands every night before our ritual margarita (or two or three.) Our casita was blown away by a hurricane a year or two later, the beach went out to sea with the casita, and Puerto Vallarta is not what it was. But neither am I.

I've been back to Puerto Vallarta a couple of more times,

but mostly I prefer to go to Zihuatanejo, also on the west coast of Mexico, where I go every chance I can. One of my favorite places in Zia is La Casa Que Canta, a wonderfully luxurious (and expensive) small hotel, but as a retiree, I can't really afford it any more.

On one trip to La Casa Que Canta, Barbara (that's the new Barbara) and I met some friends from New York City, who invited us to go deep sea fishing with them. It was a brand new experience for us. Barbara was given the first turn in the fighting chair and immediately hooked a monster-sized marlin that leaped at least twenty feet into the air and then took off with the line like a charging locomotive. With the considerable assistance of our friends, we brought the marlin up to the boat, photographed it and cut it loose, watching it sail off to the sea. It was maybe ten feet long from the tip of its bill to its tail. We celebrated this fish tale that night with ample rations of Herradura Reposada tequila (the good stuff!). As the evening wore on, the fish grew longer and longer. I hope it survived to tell its fishy little kiddies about the nice gringos who had set it free.

The King Lear Tour

I had started to live with the "new" Barbara and thought that it would be a good idea if she met my two daughters. This was a little complicated, though, because younger daughter Judy was in London enjoying junior year abroad, and daughter Amy was spending a post-graduate year in Israel. So we embarked on a tour to visit the daughters, with better results than confronted King Lear.

London was mostly uneventful. We stayed in a pleasant little hotel off of Sloane Square where I had stayed before, saw some shows in the West End, treated Judy to a couple of nice dinners and went antiquing in the area around Portobello Road. Barbara fell in love with some antique music boxes that we found in one of the shops on Portobello Road, which has since turned into an expensive little hobby.

We traveled on from London to meet Amy in Israel. She was living in Jerusalem and we decided to stay in the Intercontinental Hotel, which overlooks the old city from East Jerusalem. We knew that it was an Arab-run hotel, which we thought was OK, because Jews, particularly Israeli Jews, make terrible servants. We expected that the Arab service people would be more accommodating. What we didn't know was that the hotel was built on the site of a desecrated Jewish cemetery. Worse, it was in that very hotel that the PLO had been organized. This made for some problems, because, whenever we hailed a taxi and gave the driver the address of the Intercontinental Hotel, the driver would spit on the ground and take off like a shot, leaving us in a cloud of dust. We learned not to give the address until we were firmly seated in the back of the taxi, and prepared to weather the taxi driver's vitriol.

After visiting with Amy in Jerusalem, I wanted to show Barbara a little more of Israel, so we headed south to Elath. Aside from the startling sight of so many buxom, blonde Scandinavian women sunbathing on the beach topless, Elath didn't offer much of interest to us. I booked us on to a sailboat trip which took us out to a beautiful Crusader castle on an island, where we had some spectacular snorkeling. Later, we enjoyed a wonderful lunch of freshly caught fish, which the Israeli boat captain's wife had prepared while we swam. Israel had finally become the land of milk and honey. It was not the rich and sophisticated country that it has since become, but it was well on the way.

Our Safari

Too late in life, I had been given some very sound advice from a wise business associate: skip your second marriage and

114

go directly to your third. It would have been better advice if it had been more timely.

Barbara and I got married in 1981, with both daughters in attendance, having returned from their foreign travels. We spent a couple of lovely days, at Arthur Bloom's urging, at The Blantyre, a castle in Lenox, Massachusetts, that had been built by one of the Gilded Age magnates. Following the Blantyre stay, we had arranged to take a wedding trip to Kenya, which involved camping out in a tent in the Masai Mara. The tent came equipped with a native servant who awoke us each morning, unzipping our tent, and bringing with him a silver tray bearing a full English breakfast.

As we stepped out of our tent each morning, we could see hundreds of wildebeest and antelope grazing peacefully nearby, the occasional giraffe munching on the treetops and elephants moseying by. We were ferried around on a Land Rover each day by an otherwise unemployed white hunter (hunting having been outlawed in Kenya), to visit snoring lions, the rare leopard, ostrich, rhinoceros, jackals, baboons, hyenas and countless other species. The Land Rover could travel freely in and around the giant herd of animals, which recognized it only as another lumbering beast that had never done anyone any harm. The only danger was from the cape buffalo, who would charge a Land Rover just for the fun of it. We were also menaced by a troop of hippopotamuses when we went by foot down to the river to watch them splash around.

Occasionally, a naked Masai warrior would wander into our campground to order a beer from the bar. They were a handsome people, still living in the Stone Age, measuring their wealth in cattle, but they earned a few cents posing for pictures, which paid for the beer. Since the Masai lived in the same mud huts with their cattle, and seemed not to care about the cow dung that clung to them, they were best admired from a little distance. Interestingly, although the Masai had little sense of time, many of them sported a Timex watch, obviously a big status symbol in the Masai world. Although Kenya has had a troubled history, to us it seemed like the Garden of Eden.

The Grande Luxe Tour

In 1985, it became time to celebrate my fiftieth birthday. I owed Barbara a trip to Italy, which had been her first choice for a wedding trip when we went instead to Kenya. Since the airplane tickets were courtesy of frequent flyer mileage, we decided to splurge by booking five-star hotels. We flew to Rome and transferred immediately to a train taking us to Florence. In those days, Florence was not yet choked with tourists, and you could actually see the great art that seemed to be everywhere.

After getting our fill of Italian renaissance art in Florence, we embarked on an automobile trip through Tuscany and Umbria, mostly staying at small hotels in vineyards or in converted castles, and sampling the local vino. It was a lovely interlude, but a little on the quiet side. We longed for a little nightlife, but none was to be found in the Italian country side. In search of greener pastures, we turned our rented auto toward Venice.

We finally arrived by boat at the island on which was located the Hotel Cipriani and disembarked, but we hadn't a clue which way it was to the hotel. With the assistance of an old crone we found muttering to herself in a little alley, we eventually found the service entrance to the Cipriani. We struggled with our luggage through the fluttering laundry that was drying by the door, until a horrified hotel staff member came to our rescue. Thus began our stay at the fabled Cipriani. I should mention that the rest of our visit to Venice was fabulous, especially the calves liver. Since childhood, I have always regarded calves liver as an abomination, unfit for human consumption, but those Venetians sure can do it up gloriously. And Harry's Bar in Venice makes the only Bellini cocktail that is worth drinking.

We departed from Venice in a little grander style than had marked our arrival and drove north to Lake Como, checking in at the fabled Villa d'Este. Lake Como is gorgeous, even in those pre-George Clooney days. We tore ourselves away from the Villa d'Este just long enough to drive through the Alps to Lugano in Switzerland, admiring the breathtaking scenery along the way and envious of the brown and white cows taking their leisure in pastures by the road. Lugano is a lovely city, but one aspect of it was more than a little disconcerting. The antique shops there seemed chock-full of exquisite Judaica, finely wrought silver candelabra, ceremonial wine cups, incense boxes and the like. It requires little imagination to understand how these treasures of the Italian Jews ended up in Swiss shops.

Our Italian trip had finally drawn to a close and we drove on to the bustling city of Milan, caught our plane to New York, and consigned the grand adventure to our memories.

More about Paris

In the mid-1980s, I was blessed with a business assignment to develop a new product in partnership with the illustrious French designer Yves St. Laurent. More accurately, I was working with YSL's crafty business manager, Pierre Berge. Although YSL attended all of my working meetings with Berge, he merely sat in the room looking very bored and rarely spoke. I don't know if YSL was ill at the time, or suffering from a deep depression, or just naturally non-communicative. All I knew is that he seemed to be very strange.

Barbara traveled with me to Paris as often as her own business schedule allowed, but she wasn't all that crazy about rubbing shoulders with the very snooty French people on the Right Bank. She's more of a *Rive Gauche* kind of person. My travel partner most of the time was an effete creative director whose company was pleasant enough, but not so pleasant that I wanted to be with him every night for dinner. We made a pact that we would have dinner together only every second night, and on the other nights, we would each go our separate ways. I discovered that on the nights when he dined alone, he buried himself in his hotel room and ordered a chicken sandwich from room service, which was the only thing that he knew how to ask for in French.

On one memorable occasion, I was in a rush to get to Paris for a crucial meeting, so I booked my flight on the Concorde. Lo and behold, the most gorgeous woman that I had ever seen settled down in the seat next to me. She was tall and willowy, with beautiful features and a mass of sparkling chestnut hair. She was also a wonderfully vivacious conversationalist, and the trip was a tired businessman's fantasy. At one point, as I turned to her, inspecting her closely, I acknowledged that she looked very familiar to me. Perhaps I had met her on a previous occasion? She bristled and in a haughty voice announced, "I am Marisa Berenson!" Then she never said another word to me. When the plane landed, she hustled off without a backward glance. I had committed the ultimate gaffe of not recognizing a celebrity.

A Career Change

I'd had it with the world of advertising, the essential triviality of the work and the shallow and sometimes disagreeable people that populated that world. I didn't want to be one of those people. I had made some money and paid off the kids' college bills, so I had some choices in life. What I chose to do was go to law school, returning to Harvard for the third time, in 1986. One of the side benefits of going to law school was that the summer after my first year was free of obligations. I could travel to some of the corners of the world that I hadn't seen before. And so ensued action-packed and sometimes hair-raising adventures traveling to Japan, China, Tibet, Hong Kong, Thailand, India, Kashmir, Russia, Hungary, Austria and finally back to New York, all in just eighty days.

Buckling Down

It was then time to get serious about finishing law school and embarking on a new career as a newly minted associate at a law firm in New York City. The days of long, leisurely vacation travels were over for a while, which was no great loss, because we were kind of burnt out on traveling anyway after the long trip around the world. We did travel a bit in the next couple of years, but nothing too stimulating—a few trips to Mexico, a week in London, ten days in Portugal. The days of earning the "big bucks" in the advertising business were over, and I needed to readjust our spending priorities.

Magical Morocco

Then, after four years of laboring as an associate in a New York law firm, I figured that finally I knew enough so that I could practice law without committing daily malpractice. I also figured out that I was likely to become eligible for a partnership, if I kissed the right derrieres, when I hit my sixty-fourth birthday. Since the law firm required that partners relinquish their partnerships at age sixty-five, this didn't seem like an attractive proposition, so I cashed in my chips and formed my own boutique practice.

Clients didn't come rushing to my door at first, so we had time to travel again. We traveled a bit to Mexico, always our default location for a vacation, then in the year 2000 we decided to go to Morocco, oblivious to the gathering storm in the Islamic world. Just before Christmas and Barbara's birthday, we booked our flights to Casablanca, with a change of planes in Paris. After settling into our seats on the plane at JFK airport, our pilot came on the speaker to announce that one of the plane's toilets was malfunctioning, so the airline would roll up another plane and there would be a brief delay—nothing to be concerned about, maybe forty-five minutes at most. Six hours later, we were still in the JFK terminal, awaiting the substitute plane, while I was frantically telephoning travel agents and hotels to change our reservations in Morocco, since we would certainly miss our connecting flight from Paris to Casablanca. Since it was after midnight in New York City, I wasn't having much luck.

We had planned to stop in Paris for a few days on our way back from Morocco, but we decided to reverse field, stay in Paris over the Christmas holiday and then get to Morocco. I managed to find a telephone in the airport, called a hotel on the Left Bank that I knew, and begged for a room. My prayers were answered. The hotel greeted us warmly, for the French, and we spent a lovely couple of days in Paris. The city was emptied of all the obnoxious Parisians, who must have split for their weekend houses in the countryside to celebrate Christmas en famille, leaving us to wander around the city without having to deal with the usual rudeness of Parisians. Even the weather held up, and we were happy to forego the chilling rains that are usual in Paris in mid-winter. We celebrated Barbara's birthday at a grand restaurant near the Eiffel Tower that was devoid of tourists, something that we had never seen before in Paris.

Christmas came and went, and we finally managed to get onto a flight to Casablanca, where we were met by the car and driver/guide who would be our companion throughout Morocco. He turned out to be a terrific person, well versed in the complicated history and culture of the country. He whisked us out of Casablanca without a backward glance, never saying so, but subtly implying that Casablanca was not a safe place for tourists. We spent our first nights in Rabat, the mostly modern capital city of Morocco, where the King's palaces were well worth a visit. In Rabat we had our first dinner of tagine, the signature Moroccan stew of chicken or lamb that is invariably served with couscous. It was delicious. The word "tagine" actually refers to the conical clay dish that the stew is prepared in, but it has become the name given to the stew itself.

From Rabat, we traveled on to the city of Fez, which was steeped in ancient buildings and had a bustling souk where we could easily have gotten lost, except for the ministrations of our guide. We bought a bunch of fezzes in Fez, to bring back to our fey friends. Fez also offered us our first experience of being besieged by Arab street urchins seeking *baksheesh,* who were relentless. Nothing that we could say or do would convince them to leave us alone, but just a word from our guide and they would disappear. We stayed in a modern hotel, with a handsome bar off the lobby area. A young black musician was entertaining at a piano, and his rendition of the theme song from the movie *Casablanca* was priceless. I looked around, but Ingrid Bergman was not in evidence. Dinner that night was tagine.

From Fez, we traveled through the countryside to the Atlas Mountains, where the predominantly Arab population of the coastal cities gave way to the Berbers. It is lost in history whether the Berbers or the Jews settled in Morocco first, but it is indisputable that both were in Morocco for centuries before the Arabs arrived. The countryside was dotted with impressive Roman ruins, some with spectacular mosaics that have withstood the centuries. Atop many of the commanding hills were ancient crumbling casbahs, which are fortified structures built to protect the populace from marauding invaders. The Atlas Mountains also boast some attractive ski resorts catering to Europeans, but the skiing season had not yet begun. Dinner most nights was tagine.

As do most tourists to southern Morocco, we arranged to be

awakened one night, long before sunrise, and driven out into the desert to watch the sunrise over the endless sand dunes. Our usual guide had passed us off to another driver, who bounced us through the pitch dark night over rutted roads in a rusty Jeep, until he stopped his vehicle in the sands, stepped out of it and simply disappeared without a trace into the darkness. We freaked out. There we were, in the middle of a desert, in a strange country, without a soul around, no one knowing where we were, with scary images from *Lawrence of Arabia* flashing through our minds. As I was considering whether to try to hot-wire the Jeep, which I had never done in my life, a shadowy figure emerged from the darkness, dressed in flowing Berber robes. A quick *"Salaam aleikhem"* passed between us, he introduced himself to us as "Omar," and instructed us to follow him.

We didn't have much choice. Omar led us to the top of one of the most impressive sand dunes, which was not an easy jaunt since we kept sliding around in the shifting sands. He motioned to us to squat in the sands and pointed us toward the east, where a faint glimmer of sunlight was beginning to show. As the sun rose, the desert went from black to deep purple, then to azure, red, gold and finally it was just sand. It was spectacularly beautiful. Now that it had become broad daylight, we looked around and found that there were other tourists perched like us at the top of every nearby sand dune. Omar extracted a generous gratuity from us, he returned us to our Jeep, our missing driver suddenly materialized out of the desert and we were driven back to our hotel without incident. Dinner that night was tagine.

We drove on to Marrakech, our last stop for this trip, and checked into La Mamounia, a luxurious hotel with lavish rooms furnished in beautiful art deco style, and boasting a magnificent garden with pool-side patio bars and cafes. A short jaunt from the hotel was the gigantic central square of Marrakech, larger than St. Mark's Square in Venice and St. Peter's in Rome put together. Each night, what appeared to be the entire population of Marrakech thronged the square, interlaced with food vendors, pickpockets, acrobats, beggars, touts, tight-rope walkers, snake charmers, fortune tellers, entertainers, spice merchants, and the flotsam and jetsam of the third world. It was mesmerizing.

At the edge of the square was one of the entrances to the Marrakech souk, which was a massive tangle of narrow alleys thronged with Arab merchants of every description. At first we entered it only with our guide, because we would have been lost forever within fifty yards of the entrance. After a few days, we braved going into the souk by ourselves, but never very far. We could never have found our way out from the depths of the souk. Some of the goods were interesting, and we bought a few things, but much of the craftsmanship was of poor quality.

We learned that, traditionally, the craftsmen of Morocco were the Jews, who had populated the country ever since the destruction of the Temple in Jerusalem. The King of Morocco was revered in the Jewish community for having protected the Jews when the country was overrun by the Nazis during World War II. There were well-kept Jewish synagogues and cemeteries scattered about, but there were no Jews. The Jewish community had not been threatened by the Arabs, but after the Six Day War, the Jews became nervous and quietly slipped away, the wealthy to France, Canada or the United States, the poor to Israel. Sadly, Morocco lost its middle class and its traditions of fine craftsmanship, and the Jews lost another ancient homeland.

By the time we got to Marrakech, we had had enough tagine to last us for the rest of our lives. Not that it was ever less than tasty, but enough is enough. Fortunately, Marrakech is blessed with a number of fine French restaurants, many serving the old-fashioned style of French food, dripping with rich sauces, that has pretty well disappeared from Paris, but that I adore. I was in heaven. We had been cautioned, though, not to miss having dinner at Yacout, deep in the heart of the souk, and that advice was sound.

Through our hotel's concierge, we made a dinner reservation at Yacout, and we were instructed to take a small taxi to the restaurant. As an aside, Marrakech taxis come in two sizes, for reasons that shortly became apparent. As darkness fell, our small taxi plunged into the souk until the alleys became so narrow that it could go no further. A "large" taxi wouldn't have stood a chance. We paid the driver, exited the taxi, and were greeted by a little Arab boy carrying a lantern. We followed him a hundred yards to the door of a nondescript building, which, upon our entering, revealed itself to be the restaurant. The interior was spectacularly beautiful, done in haute-Oriental style, with gorgeous silk pillows piled on lavish sofas, and beaten brass lamps illuminating the scene.

We were ushered to the roof of the building for cocktails and to see the souk and the surrounding city of Marrakech spread out before us, with its lights sparkling like jewels lying on black velvet. A cliché, I know, but that is exactly what it looked like. Somewhere in the distance we heard the sounds of a muezzin proclaiming in Arabic that God is great. For a moment, we could agree. After a suitable interval, we were led to our table and served an endless array of appetizers, perhaps twenty dishes in all, accompanied by red and white wines. Then the main courses began to arrive, including the omnipresent tagine, but others as well. The dinner concluded with sticky desserts in the Middle-Eastern style. I've had better food, including some of the French food in Marrakech, but I've never dined in such a spectacular setting.

Morocco was a fascinating trip, layered as it is with the cultures of ancient Greece and Rome, the Berbers, the Jews, the Arabs, Spain, France and even central Africa. They have all left their imprint.

The AZA Excursion

My high school buddies, egged on by Arthur Bloom and his wife Deborah, organized a reunion and group trip to visit Arthur in Paris and Normandy, where Arthur now lived. We joined them with a bit of trepidation, because we did not usually travel in a group, preferring to do things our own way and at our own pace. Even though most of us had gone to the same college, I hadn't seen much of these guys, except for Arthur, since high school. There was no good reason for this separation, it was just one of those things that happened along the way, as we all built careers, had families and scattered to take up residences along the East Coast. Nonetheless, we all melded into a happy traveling group, including the wives, whom I mostly was meeting for the first time.

Ray Leiter was there, a bit balder and with a scraggily beard, but not much changed in his slightly off-center personality from the last time that I had seen him, probably in 1956. His wacky but wise sense of humor was a constant source of surprise.

Of course, Arthur Bloom, our host, was there, proudly showing off Paris, his adopted city. Arthur had fled New York and the Berkshires from a distinguished career in academia to live in Paris and to write a novel. I had seen Arthur from time to time over the years, so I was prepared for the "new" Arthur, so different from the Arthur of fifty years ago or even twenty years ago. No longer the serious and diligent young guy I once knew, he had become a *flaneur* and Parisian *roué.*

Zummie Katz was there also, still of the twinkling eye and gentle manner, perhaps the least changed of any of us by the intervening years. Since Zummie had gone off to Yale to attend college, while the rest of us had the good sense to go to Harvard, I hadn't seen him since Latin School graduation in 1952. It was my loss.

Marty Mintz was there, with a halo of thinning, white hair,

and the same puckish manner that I remembered from the fifties. Marty hadn't changed at all in personality, which is a good thing.

Don Orenbuch was there, a towering fountain of knowledge in such diverse subjects as military history and Japanese flower arranging. I hadn't remembered that Donnie had such wide-ranging interests, which were a constant amazement.

Arnie Abelow was there, perhaps the quietest of this sometimes rowdy group, but quick with his sharp wit when the occasion arose. When Arnie and Marty would get together to reprise one of their comedy routines, it was priceless.

The last member of the group was Paul Rosenthal, quiet and serious as ever. Paul's family had recently suffered an awful tragedy, and Paul and his wife were struggling to put it behind them, but it was difficult for them. It was wonderful that they made the brave effort to join in the festivities.

We all had a great time together and promised to do it again soon. A couple of years later, Arthur and Deborah exchanged their apartment in St. Germain en Laye and the *moulin* in Normandy with us to take up residence in our apartment in Manhattan and our home in the Hamptons for three weeks. Sadly, our trip to Arthur's homes in France was interrupted by news of Barbara's father's terminal illness, which demanded our immediate return to the States. We'll do it again one day.

The Glorious Nation of Kazakhstan

Daughter Amy had been struggling for a couple of years to adopt a baby and finally learned that a little girl had been found for her, requiring her to travel to the remote city of Karaganda in the far reaches of Kazakhstan to retrieve the baby. I wasn't about to let my little girl (she was about forty-six years old at the time) go off to this strange and distant destination all by herself, so I agreed to accompany her.

The trickiest part of preparing for the journey was pulling together about $12,000 in green, folding cash to take with us for the various fees and expenses required in connection with the adoption. Apparently, Kazakhstan doesn't have much of a banking system, and cash rules. Moreover, the cash had to be in the form of brand-new, uncirculated bills, because there is a huge problem of counterfeit money circulating in the countries of the former Soviet Union, so specie has to be run through handy machines that detect counterfeits. Unfortunately, these same machines will kick out any bills that show the slightest imperfection. Hence the need for uncirculated bills. Amy was in a panic, because our trip was just two days away, and so far she had assembled only 100 newly printed one-dollar bills. I said that I would take care of it. But how?

My local banks weren't much help because apparently little in the way of new bills was available on short notice due to the season of the year. It was summer, and the Federal Reserve Board was drawing down the supply of cash in the system, not shipping out new bills to the banks. I phoned every lawyer that I knew who had banking clients. They went to work on their clients right away, but nothing materialized. In desperation, I called my old college roommate, Ed Furash, who had been a consultant to banks for many years but was now retired. Ed didn't think he could help, but I pleaded, "Ed, I've known you for fifty years, and I've never asked you for a favor. I'm on my knees begging; I need this money!" Ed never could stand tears. He said he'd get back to me. Sure enough, Ed came through an hour later, instructing me to go see "Susan" at the nearby head-quarters of Citibank, where the bills would be waiting for me. Of course, Citibank was the first place that I had gone in my search, where I was told that my requirements were impossible. Ed pulled the right string.

Daughter Amy and I set off a day later on our journey to the East, stopping for a day in Frankfurt to rest along the way.

I carried the money with me wrapped in a brown paper bag, hoping that it would pass for my lunch in case anyone looked in my carry-on. Twelve thousand dollars in bills makes quite an impressive stack.

The following day, we flew from Frankfurt to Almaty, the principal city of Kazakhstan. The flight was very long and we arrived exhausted, so we didn't look around very much before crashing in the apartment that the adoption agency had provided for us. Almaty appeared to be a substantial city, with a number of modern buildings and luxury shops catering mostly to the Westerners who were swarming into Kazakstan to exploit its massive oil and gas reserves. The following morning, we headed back to the airport for our flight to Karaganda, still hours away. The flight was on an ancient and rickety prop plane, most likely left over from World War II, so we rejoiced when we finally touched down in Karaganda, to be met by our car and driver, and an interpreter. They greeted us warmly and drove us over deeply rutted roads to the apartment that would be our home for the next three weeks.

Let's be kind: the apartment was a hovel, located in a grim courtyard, usually occupied by sullen men sitting on benches swigging from vodka bottles and muttering darkly to each other. The road leading to our apartment was riddled by potholes, some of which would have challenged a Soviet tank. The entranceway to the apartment was dark and unlit, with trash strewn around and an accumulation of decades of grime on every surface. The apartment itself was passably clean, with electricity that usually worked and an unreliable hot water heater that seemed to have a rhythm of its own. There was a minimal kitchen equipped with a few dishes, some pots and pans, an electric stove and a surprisingly efficient small refrigerator. We could manage.

There was an old desktop computer sitting on a table in the living room, but I had little hope that it would actually work.

I idly flicked the switch to turn it on, and to my surprise it responded. In a few minutes I was connected to the internet and a minute later I was e-mailing Barbara. God bless Bill Gates, Al Gore and whoever else invented the internet! Although we were ten thousand miles from home, we were connected to the world.

Our first stop was to head to the baby house. It is called a baby house and not an orphanage because many of the children who are living there are not orphans. Their parents might be in prison, or suffering from some serious illness, or the children might have been abandoned by their parents because of a cleft lip or other deformities. There was a mob of little tykes living in the baby house, ranging from infants to toddlers, all clean, well dressed and in apparent good health. They were cared for by matronly Russian women, who seemed devoted to their work, and genuinely caring about the children. Maybe this baby house was a Potemkin showplace organized for the benefit of Westerners, but we were impressed.

A word about the ethnic groups in Karaganda: Most of the population were Russians, who had dominated the country since the time that it had been part of the Soviet Union. The Kazakhs, a distinctly Oriental-featured people, were a minority in their own country. Formerly a nomadic people, their culture (and their cuisine) centered around horses. The third most populous ethnic group, mysteriously, were Koreans. I tried to find out why there seemed to be so many Koreans and learned that Karaganda had been the administrative center of the Gulag during Soviet days. Its population had been a diverse collection of nationalities transported there from throughout the Soviet Union and its satellites. When the Soviet Union fell apart, much of the population returned to their native countries, abandoning the harsh life of Kazakhstan, but the Koreans remained because they had no place else to go.

I won't go in detail into the misadventures that attended our finally adopting the beautiful and brilliant Leah. She is now a treasured part of our family, but things didn't go smoothly at first. At one point Amy and I were close to returning to New York empty-handed, our mission a failure. Eventually the problems got sorted out, but not without some drama and heartache. It was more than worth it, though.

I stayed in Karaganda for three weeks with Amy, who by then had moved into a more comfortable hotel to stay for an additional three weeks. When I left Amy in Karaganda, to meet Barbara in Paris for a previously planned vacation, things in Karaganda seemed well under control. Amy had connected with the local Jewish population, with her skills at languages she had picked up enough Russian to get by, and she had even developed a tolerance for the bleak Kazakh food (but never for horsemeat). When Amy finally returned to New York, she was accompanied by the best travel souvenir anyone ever had.

Turning Seventy

With all this flitting around the globe, there are still lots of places that I've never been, some of which are on my list for future excursions. So when my big birthday rolled around, Barbara asked me where I would like to go. Maybe to Greece and Turkey? Or how about Rio de Janeiro and Buenos Aires? I decided that I would prefer to gather a few close friends and travel to Brighton Beach in Brooklyn, to celebrate at one of the Russian nightclubs that have sprung up in the midst of the thriving Russian immigrant community. Barbara was a little skeptical, but launched into the planning of this big event with a semblance of good cheer.

With some help from a Russian coworker, Barbara had little difficulty in choosing the venue, but she decided to journey out to the wilds of Brighton Beach to check out the nightclub's menu. She knows very well how important food is to me. Anyway, the menu seemed reasonable to Barbara, with a choice of perhaps a dozen hot and cold appetizers, five or six main courses, a number of desserts and a special Russian birthday cake. We would not starve. The management of the club threw in a supply of vodka as part of the deal, and we were encouraged to bring our own wine. We would not be thirsty, either.

On the appointed night, our friends gathered first at our apartment for champagne and caviar, and we were already more than a little looped when we set off on our journey to Brooklyn. We had arranged for one of those prom night stretch limousines to transport us on our way, so we all piled in, delighted to find that the limousine was equipped with a well-stocked bar. We tottered into the nightclub and were shown to our table toward the rear of a large room, graced with a dance floor and a stage for the orchestra and the entertainment to come. For those with long memories, the club looked very much like the old Aperion Plaza in Roxbury, with lots of crystal chandeliers, lots of velvet draperies, and gilded mirrors decorating every wall. The other tables were packed with beefy Russian men in tight-fitting suits and their equally beefy wives, all dressed to kill. It was a boisterous crowd, definitely out looking for a good time. We fit right in.

As we settled in at our table, we realized that Barbara had misunderstood the menu; we were not to have a choice of the dozen or so appetizers, we would have them all. Food started arriving from every direction until the large table could accommodate no more. Still it came, until we begged for mercy. There were tureens of borscht, platters of smoked fishes, piles of pelmeni, mountains of pickled herring, tubs of potatoes, salads galore, it was obscene. We fressed until we could fress no more. Then the main courses arrived, all of the main courses. There was chicken, there was fish, there was beef, there was veal. We plotzed.

At two in the morning, the waiters were still bringing piles of food.

There was dancing, of course, and Barbara cut a mean rug with a very buxom woman at the next table. In between the orchestra's sets, the master of ceremonies, looking like a cross between Wayne Newton and Reggie von Gleason, was regaling us with what seemed to be a comedy routine, lost on us since it was all in Russian. He introduced the entertainers, singers of soulful Russian ballads, energetic acrobatic dancers in skimpy outfits, and a particularly memorable violinist who played a pretty fair version of "The Flight of the Bumble Bees," enlivened by a projection of manic bumble bees disporting on a screen behind him.

As we started thinking that it might be time to leave, while we still could walk, the master of ceremonies started chanting "Jerry! Jerry! Jerry!" and the whole club took up the call. I figured that he must mean me, so I grabbed Barbara and we went up to the stage, while one of the skimpily clad acrobatic dancers wheeled a huge birthday cake, ablaze with candles, over to me. Barbara and I blew out the candles, the crowd sang "Happy Birthday" in Russian, and we returned to our table to deal with the desserts that were now arriving for us from every direction. Enough was enough, we fled the club to our waiting limousine, closely followed by packs of waiters bearing bundles of pastries.

It was a great birthday celebration, and I plan to do it again when I turn eighty. You're all invited, especially the cardiologists among you.

CHAPTER SEVEN

Dick Savrann

I WAS BORN JULY 28, 1935, at the Boston City Hospital. My parents, Abraham and Doris, were living in Roxbury at Nazing Court. My father was a cartoonist at the *Boston Traveler* and my mother was a housewife.

My father was brought to this country from a shtetl called Sovrun on the Russian-Polish border in 1904, when he was either four or six, depending on who told the story. He grew up in East Cambridge and graduated from Rindge Tech High School in Cambridge having "majored" in art and drafting. He got a job at the *Boston Post* newspaper, where he was allowed to finish and embellish cartoons by other artists. In World War II he entered the army but the Armistice occurred while he was still in training. After he was mustered out, he went to work as a cartoonist at the *Boston Traveler.* He shortened (changed) his name from Savransky to Savrann at the behest of his bosses at the paper; later, he adopted "SAV" as a shorthand signature on his cartoons. He became known as Sav for the rest of his life.

My mother was native-born in Boston in 1910. She grew up in New Bedford, Oak Bluffs, and East Boston. Her family name was Curhan, later changed to Cohen, and then changed back again to Curhan, for reasons that remain unclear to me.

One of my earliest recollections is of looking from a bed through a window at my grandmother and an aunt, who were waving to me through a window from the front steps of the building in which we lived. I later learned that I was about three at the time and was suffering from a strep infection, because of which nobody was allowed to visit.

I don't remember much more from the days at Nazing Court.

My younger, and only brother, Arnold, was born in 1937. The family relocated to 4 Elm Hill Park, also in Roxbury, before the Second World War. Jerry Davidow lived on Elm Hill Avenue, which was almost directly across Warren Street from my home. I recall being in his house at an early age, perhaps five or six. I remember that on one occasion he showed me a fetus in a jar of formaldehyde that he had uncovered in his physician father's home study.

I attended the William Lloyd Garrison Elementary School, which was near Franklin Park and a good uphill hike from where I lived. I vaguely recall walking up the hill, but I also recall being driven to school along with friends most mornings. At the Garrison, as we called it, I was put into a rapid advancement program and had a Miss White (whom I was quite enamored of) for three years. I did grades two through five in two years, along with about twenty-five other kids. Most of the kids in "rapid advancement" were Jewish. I did well and graduated from the program, placing me (unhappily) with bigger, more mature, and more athletic kids for the rest of my academic career.

The playground at the Garrison was a lively place. The Jewish boys would trade stamps and coins while the others roughhoused. I had an uncle who lived in Gloucester, who was in the stamp business, and I was always sending off for stamps "on approval," so I was very busy trading stamps on the playground. Occasionally, my father brought me to some coin stores around

Bromfield Street in Boston, where I would pore over the ten-cent items and on occasion would get a better piece. To this day, I have kept my coin collection. My children and grandchildren have failed to see any romance in collecting old coins.

There were some older boys who lived on Elm Hill Park and they would teach me some rudiments of throwing and catching a football. There were lively touch football games in the street, with the curbs being the sidelines. My father was athletic and would sometimes join the games and show off his drop-kicking skill, which was considerable.

When war broke out, the older neighborhood boys all left for the service. My Uncle Lou, or Sonny as we all called him, was living with my mother's parents and two of his sisters on Fayston Street, about a mile or two away from Elm Hill Park, and he would come over to our house almost every week night to play cards with my father, chess with me, or a game in which we rolled a wooden ball into depressions on a board with my dad and my younger brother. Sonny started attending signal corps school at night at a local elementary school (the Lewenberg) and I remember seeing all the students playing ball in the school yard before going in to class in the early evening.

When Uncle Sonny left for the service (in the signal corps), his Studebaker was kept in a garage beside our house until he was discharged in 1945. My mother did not have a license but did take driving lessons and obtained one in 1945. I remember that the first time she drove my brother and me to the traditional Friday evening dinner at my grandmother's house, she pulled out from the curb without looking and slightly side-swiped a passing car. It was a source of some embarrassment but she got over it and became a fine driver.

I guess the world was more trusting then, because I remember my father giving a few dollars to some older unemployed guys, who would congregate at our local drugstore, to take me to a Red Sox game with them. To this day I remember going to see an afternoon game with these virtual strangers in which Mel Parnell pitched for the Sox. I must have been about ten, placing this in 1945. Of course I became a lifelong Red Sox fan. I recall my father taking me to see the All Star game at Fenway Park in 1946, in which Ted Williams hit his famous home run into the bull pen off Rip Sewell's "blooper ball," and to a World Series game also pitched by Mel Parnell that same year. To this day, I have saved the programs that I got at those games, and even now my front license plate says "Boston Red Sox."

Every Friday we would go to my maternal grandma's for a family dinner. I would help her with the "lochshin" (noodles) and would hand roll cigarettes for my grandfather. He would light one and the tobacco would fall out due to my poor workmanship, whereupon he would lecture me on the fine art of rolling a cigarette (which I have never forgotten).

I was at my grandmother's house early one Friday afternoon when my cousin Stan (Sanford Larkin) returned from three years in the army, having been wounded at Guadalcanal and spending about a year in hospitals on the West Coast and Philadelphia. I can still visualize the whole hysterical scene with my grandmother, as there was no advance notice of his arrival home and she and I were, for some reason, alone at the time.

During the war, my Aunt Ida, one of my mother's sisters who was living with my grandparents, would take me to see a vaudeville show and movie in downtown Boston on a Saturday afternoon. I was about seven to ten years old. We would sit in the balcony (usually the second balcony) and after the show she would treat me to an ice cream at Bailey's or Schrafft's, and then we would take the subway and a streetcar back to Roxbury. I loved those outings.

Also during the war my father worked for the OPA (Office of Price Administration) and the defense department, drawing posters such as "Uncle Sam Wants You!" and "Loose Lips Sink Ships." Today, the originals are quite valuable but we do not have any of them in the family. Despite his honorable discharge in World War I there was no record of my father as a citizen, so he had to be made one before he could begin work as an artist for the government. I remember him calling himself a "ninety-day wonder," as he was made a citizen in ninety days.

My dad then had another job doing publicity for the Suffolk Downs race track. He would take my brother and me there for the day and we would go into the jockey room, watch the photographer develop prints of close finishes, and watch the horses in the paddock area. This was his version of being a babysitter. He got my cousin Stan a job parking VIP cars at the track once Stan was discharged from the service. There evidently was no lasting effect, as gambling has never had any particular appeal for me.

We moved to Dorchester in 1946. Our new house was a fifty-year-old Victorian on Thames Street near Codman Square. This was not a Jewish area, and the adjacent Park Street was "lace curtain" Irish. We had pretty nice neighbors, except for the Buckleys who were next door. The old man was a terrible drunk and the kids had to go look for him on payday and drag him out of some bar. Often we observed a cab pulling up, and he would be unceremoniously dumped unconscious on his front porch. However, we kept our distance and had little to do with the Buckleys.

Two or three streets away from Thames Street was Millet Street, where some Jewish kids lived. I made a few good friends on Millet Street, although they went to a different school. I attended the Nightingale School in the sixth grade. One day each week, my class of boys had to take "shop" (woodworking) at another school in a much tougher area about two miles away. After class, we would be subjected to taunts, many of them anti-Semitic, and would have to sneak home. Sometimes, we would get caught and punched around for being Jewish, or "fags." One time, we had to run a gauntlet to escape the school yard. Luckily, there never were any serious injuries. Nevertheless we were terrified on the days we had to walk to and from the other school. There was never a teacher or administrator in sight once the bell rang.

My brother and I were started on piano lessons by our Aunt Gertrude from Brookline. We had an upright in a small study on the second floor. After one year, I was politely asked to take up something else. My brother continued and eventually became a pretty good pianist, who would play before assemblies at Latin School when he was only a "Sixie" (seventh grader).

My father continued working as a cartoonist for advertising agencies and became an assistant publicity and advertising director for the Harvard Athletic Association. Starting in the thirties he had drawn original covers for the Harvard football programs (as well as some other schools) and before long I went to the Harvard games with him, sat in the press box, and became a big fan. One year, he brought my brother and me to the Yale game (when it meant something in sports) and left us in two stadium seats while he went to the press box. Luckily for us, my cousin Merle, who was attending with a date, saved us from frostbite by covering us with a blanket when the temperature dropped precipitously and it started to snow. I believe Eli Jackson was the big star of the game playing for Yale that day.

I attended the Oliver Wendell Holmes Junior High School in the seventh and eighth grades. The school population mirrored the neighborhood, with even one or two blacks. We all seemed to get along all right and I don't recall any problems of note. The school had an old wooden annex where printing was still taught to the boys. I took printing as an elective and can remember the layout of the building to this day. We printed school announcements, invitations, etc. Later, the annex was torn down and the vacant area became an informal playground featuring basketball. The neighborhood kids set up a backboard and net each day and took it down after play. It was stored in our cellar.

My father was a golf fanatic and as kids, my brother and I and half the neighborhood would play our own version of miniature golf in our backyard with our friends. One day an old man appeared from the next yard and handed us an armful of antique golf clubs over the fence, explaining that he had been a caddy at Carnoustie in Scotland and brought the clubs with him to the States. We used the old clubs, but unfortunately they were left behind when we moved again, to Brookline. Those clubs would all be museum pieces today.

After doing well at the "Ollie," as our school was called by its pupils, I was allowed to transfer into Boston Latin School without taking an entrance exam. I entered "Latin" as a ninth grader in 1948. My father generally drove a group of kids to school each morning, very rare in those days, and my mother would pick us up. It sure beat using the "T."

During my tenure at Latin School, I joined the AZA. My sole motive was social. There were dances with B'nai B'rith girls and basketball, at which I played assiduously but not too well. I never made the school basketball team, although I tried out a few times. Many of the kids I met in AZA went on to Harvard and remain friends to this day. I recall our "field trips" to esoteric locales such as Revere and Malden. If we made dates with any of the girls we met at the dances, we generally ended up at the Totem Pole Ballroom in Newton ("swing and sway with Sammy Kaye") or at a movie.

I liked Latin School, made a lot of friends, and learned a little Latin and Ancient Greek. I joined the golf team, made captain in my senior year and was lucky enough to win the City of Boston high school championship, despite there being better players in the field. Mr. Dunn, our librarian, but actually college advisor, "proposed" (tantamount to admission) that I apply to Harvard, where I was one of ninety-odd students to matriculate in the fall of 1952. I was sixteen when I graduated Latin and seventeen when I entered Harvard on a partial scholarship and grant-in-aid.

By this time, my folks had sold the house in Dorchester and bought one in South Brookline. I commuted to college my freshman year and then moved into Adams House for my sophomore year. I majored in soc-relations at Harvard, called by all "soc rel," which included sociology, psychology, and anthropology. My roommate, Irving Zola (a fellow AZA-er), also majored in soc rel and we wrote a joint paper for Professor Clyde Kluckhorn in an introductory physical anthropology course. Irv did the research and I wrote the paper and we got an A. Irv went on to become a sociology professor at Brandeis, but after my senior thesis was handed in (an analysis of reaction to types of humorous cartoons by social class), I lost interest in pursuing any part of "soc rel."

My years at Harvard were busy and enjoyable. I always had a part-time job. I knew a lot of kids from Latin School and Adams House, as well as from clubs I had joined and the golf teams, on which I played for three years. I was fairly studious but not overly so. I always had an old but serviceable car, gifts from my Uncle Sonny who had become an automobile dealer together with cousin Stan in 1946. I worked for him in the summer, and every day at about 3:00 p.m. he would tell me to get my clubs and we would go over to Ponkapoag Golf Course, about ten minutes from his Chevy dealership in Randolph, for a quick nine holes. Once he brought me to a Chevy dealers outing and palmed me off as his assistant. I won the low gross that day and my uncle took a lot of good natured heat from the other dealers for bringing a "ringer." As a prize, they gave me a set of kids' clubs (which I immediately sold).

In my senior year at Harvard, I started dating my wife to be. I had met her a year earlier when three members of the Harvard golf team traveled to Haverhill to join our captain, Bob Ornsteen, for a round at his country club. After we played eighteen holes, Bobby Stone left because he had a date that night, Roger Fleischman and I decided to play nine more holes, and Bob inveigled Diane to join us as a fourth. She later said she was intimidated, but I don't recall that being the case. She played pretty well. When I asked her where she went to school and she answered "Sophie Newcomb" in New Orleans, I bid adieu. When Bob Ornsteen called me the following year to tell me that the girl who played golf with us had transferred to Brandeis and offered her phone number, I enlisted my good friend at Harvard (although a Boston English grad) Lenny Singer to join me on a double date. Whichever girl, Diane or her roommate, opened the door would be his date. It worked out, although later I realized that when I called to arrange the date, Diane had mixed me up with my teammate Roger Fleischman, who was not only better looking but a much better golfer. I hope she wasn't too disappointed.

I had intended to go to business school after graduating from college, and applied to and was admitted to Columbia but turned down at Harvard. However, as matters became interesting between Diane and me, I applied to the law school at literally the last minute. I commuted from Brookline my first year. Diane and I were married during the Christmas break of 1957, in my second year. Diane became a student teacher in Belmont, having graduated from Brandeis, and obtained a master's degree from the Harvard Graduate School of Education. We rented an apartment in Belmont and took some evening meals at my law school club near the school. I recall that dinner was $1.05 at the club and that we had to pay with coupons.

Diane became pregnant, and barely made it through the school year undiscovered. Her last report noted that her dress had become "sloppy." I graduated from Harvard Law in June 1959 with an undistinguished, but better than average record. I never felt entirely comfortable at the law school. I had little interest in practicing law when I graduated except as a means to make a living. When one professor of note told me, when I complained about a low grade, that I suffered from "gaps," and I asked him what he meant, he said, "Gaps in your knowledge; they are considerable." I had worked in a law firm in Boston after my junior year, and although I liked the atmosphere, I found the work repetitive and unexciting. That summer was one of the last in which lawyers were still expected to wear a flat-top straw hat on the streets, and the courts were closed (except for emergencies). I actually bought a straw hat and wore it to work on the trolley from our apartment in Belmont.

When my father-in-law offered me the chance to go to work for him in the shoe business (at double my highest offer from a respected downtown law firm) I opted to become a junior executive and learn the business. Diane and I had bought a small house with our wedding presents and moved to Andover in 1958, while I was still a student. We had been forced to move from our apartment by a landlady who did not appreciate our new dog. I drove to Cambridge every day on old Route 28 before Interstate 93 was opened. In November 1958, our first son was born, and I was a homeowner, husband, father, dog owner, part-time tax preparer, and commuter-student, as I stumbled through to graduation day. A well-paying job and a new vista seemed attractive at the time. Little could I know that the best days of the domestic shoe manufacturing business were coming to an end and that within twenty years shoe manufacturing would barely exist in New England.

I stayed in the shoe business for almost four years. I found it fascinating at first. I guess that I was always a businessman at heart. I did get involved in some legal and political issues, as imports were starting to compete with domestic manufacturers and there was a lot of protectionist sentiment as the manufacturers lobbied for support in Washington. That didn't happen except for some requirements of labeling that were thought to impact more on cheap imports made of synthetic leather than on the so-called quality products made in the USA. I wonder if the labeling accomplished anything for the consumer or for the industry.

Unfortunately, when one of the factories managed by the family needed a new general manager, I was disappointed not even to be seriously considered for the position. In retrospect, I was dreaming when I imagined that I was qualified. That, plus a difficult personal situation that developed between one of my bosses and me, led to my walking out of the shoe business without notice one sunny afternoon and heading to a local golf course instead of staying at my desk. I never even returned for my rubber-soled work shoes.

I was twenty-eight years old, unemployed with two kids. I decided that my options were pretty limited and I may as well try to be a lawyer. With no experience, and having to compete with new grads, I was not a very desirable product. The big firms didn't want me competing with their new hires, and small firms were leery of a Harvard Law graduate who would deign to work for them. I had an interview with my father-in-law's law firm, Sullivan & Worcester, where John Worcester advised me to hang out a shingle, like he did, and go it alone.

Through the Harvard Law School placement office I found a job with a young entrepreneurial lawyer and developer, Jerome L. Rappaport. He was only seven years my senior but had already made a name for himself in Democratic politics, was married to the niece of the mayor of Boston, and involved in redevelopment of Boston's West End. "Jerry" had a small law office and needed an associate to replace one who was leaving. The job paid little, but I could keep fifty percent of whatever fees I generated on my own. It worked out well, as I was fortunate to find business come my way. When the associate who had left came back, I was retained. We were a firm of three associates and one proprietor. Phil Howorth went on to become a judge in New Hampshire, and Dan Rakov sadly lost his life after a swimming mishap.

We "specialized" in eminent domain cases, brought on by the redevelopment of Boston's Scollay Square and the Faneuil Hall market district, and in relocation of the businesses forced to move from those areas. The work was interesting and profitable for the firm. After a few years Ed Newell joined us as an associate specializing in eminent domain trial work. To this day, I am in contact with Ed, who now lives in Charlotte, North Carolina.

In the early sixties, I was invited to attend a meeting of the Andover Republican Club. I became fascinated by and became involved in politics. I worked closely with Eliot Richardson when he ran for attorney general of Massachusetts. I considered myself a moderate Republican, of which we had a long tradition in the state, going back to Senator Leverett Saltonstall and including Governor Francis Sargent, Lt. Governor Frank Hatch and Richardson (later to become famous for quitting rather than firing the special prosecutor in the Watergate affair). When he was elected, Richardson offered me an assistant attorney generalship. I chose to join the eminent domain division where for two years I tried many jury cases for the Commonwealth, including a few very large and interesting ones.

In 1968, Richardson asked me to do him a favor by working for Richard Nixon in his presidential campaign. He had promised to supply somebody who was politically oriented. I agreed and spent four-plus months campaigning full-time ("United Citizens for Nixon-Agnew"). The present campaigns look the same to me, except for the spending of much more money. Diane and I attended the inauguration and inaugural balls and the new President gave me a set of gold presidential cufflinks, which I still have in a drawer somewhere. Although I was being promoted by Senator Ed Brooke, Richardson and others with whom I worked on the campaign for a position in the new administration, Diane and I ultimately decided to stay in Boston. We had just finished constructing and decorating a new house, the kids were small, and Washington held little allure for us at the time.

In 1970 I left the attorney general's office, Richardson having gone on to Washington, and I opened a new firm with another assistant attorney general, Howard Miller (now living and still working in Martha's Vineyard) and my old associate Ed Newell. In one form or another that firm persisted for over twenty years, growing to about twenty-four lawyers at its zenith.

In 1971, Howard Miller and I represented Governor Sargent in defense of a "ten taxpayer" redistricting lawsuit before the Supreme Judicial Court. Defending the state senate alongside us was James St. Clair, who later represented Richard Nixon in the days leading up to the impeachment vote. We managed to convince the justices that the governor was blameless, and he was dismissed from the suit.

In 1972, Howard ran for Congress as a moderate Republican and anti-Vietnam War candidate. I acted as his campaign treasurer and general advisor. He was defeated by Joseph Moakley, who went on to serve in the House for about thirty years with great distinction.

In the meanwhile, Diane and I continued to live in Andover with our two sons. Both of the boys attended the Pike School, a private elementary school where classes were small, and they then went on to boarding schools, Stephen to Middlesex, and the younger Russell to Governor Dummer Academy. Stephen graduated from Babson and is now a vice president of UBS in Boston. He and Michelle have three kids: Jessica, a senior at the University of Vermont; Danielle, a sophomore at Endicott; and Andrew. Russell graduated from Emory University and Suffolk Law, worked for my firm for a while and then for my former partner Howard Miller for a few years, and eventually became an associate general counsel of Starwood Hotels. He is now a name partner in Sandman/Savrann, a national firm specializing in hotel and hospitality law. He lives in Guilford, Connecticut, with his wife, Jen, and daughters, Elizabeth, a sophomore at Oberlin, and Lindsay.

In 1973, Diane and I took the boys on a seven-week motor trip around the country. We put almost 10,000 miles on our Country Squire. A high point of the trip was our experience with a "flying saucer" in the desert of Arizona, where we had driven to take photographs of a sunset. As a result of our reporting what we saw, we were required to submit our photos and to answer a lengthy questionnaire for some federal agency, from whom we never heard again.

Governor Sargent asked me to recommend someone to be appointed as a member of my local housing authority in 1972. The Andover Housing Authority managed old "veteran housing," elderly housing, and subsidized rentals for persons of low income. I did not come up with a clear choice, so he appointed me. When my appointed term ended, I ran for one of the elective positions on the authority, was elected, and eventually remained in that office for sixteen straight years, as chairman for the last seven. In my tenure, we built two new projects for the elderly, a total of about 300 apartments, and a group home for retarded adults. At one time we also managed 300 apartments under "Section 8" federal subsidies.

I became involved in some other community projects. I served for years on both the board of the ABC ("A Better Chance") and the Hospice of the Merrimack Valley (along with my wife Diane, who actually helped to start the hospice) and later served as president for a year. The hospice became one of the largest in New England, and it was very gratifying to us to see it grow. Also, I was president of the Harvard Club of Andover for about twenty years, which led me to having the honor and fun of representing Harvard at the installations of two presidents at nearby colleges—Merrimack College and

Bradford College. As Harvard was the oldest college present, I led the academic processions into the hall, bedecked in a robe—supplied by Harvard—befitting my doctorate (JD) status. For once, Yale trailed behind me. I also served as a trustee and secretary of the Boston Latin School Foundation for close to ten years and enjoyed helping in a small way the school achieve better physical facilities and more stable funding. We had to deal with the Boston School Committee and Boston City Hall, as well as two complex federal lawsuits concerning admissions policies. It certainly was illuminating. Latin School is one of Boston's finest institutions and merits, in my view, all the help its alumni can provide.

In 1992, our old law firm broke up as a casualty of the banking crisis, and I joined Burns & Levinson along with Mike Goshko, one of my partners. B&L had 115 lawyers and was a strong regional firm representing mostly small and medium-sized businesses. One of my former partners there is now sitting on the Supreme Judicial Court of Massachusetts. I remained at B&L for seven years, leaving to join a smaller firm, where I would not be required to submit "business plans" that would never be read or implemented. In 1986 I had begun to commute to Florida in the wintertime, as Diane found the warm weather necessary for health reasons. The small firm allowed me more freedom to come and go as I pleased.

In 2005, Diane and I finally decided to move to Florida full time. The commuting was becoming impossible to bear after 9/11 and we had to make a choice. Fortunately, I was already a member of the Florida Bar. I opened a small practice while acting as in-house counsel to a friend's financial sector business. I thought that I would work a few days and play golf a few days. However, I find that I am going in to the office virtually every day, and playing golf only occasionally (and usually poorly). We have made a lot of good friends here, and although we still think of "home" as Massachusetts, we are not going back. Walking outside at 9:00 p.m. in February and March and finding sixty-eight-degree weather is too nice to give up.

I suppose my life would have been quite different if I had gone to (Columbia) Business School instead of the (Harvard) Law School, if I had gone to work in a law firm instead of a shoe factory, if I had taken a job in the Nixon administration instead of staying in Boston, etc., etc. But I feel that the end result is perfectly acceptable. I am fortunate to have been married to the same lovely woman for over fifty years; to have two productive and happily married kids and five nice grandkids; to live in a nice community; and to still be in decent shape. Now, if only I could figure out what is wrong with my golf swing.

CHAPTER EIGHT

Ray Leiter

I. Forgiveness

BY NOW YOU'VE READ several chapters devoted to telling you how wonderful the Haym Salomon chapter of AZA was, how it helped shape our lives, how great it was to see one another at our reunions. How cloying; worse, how inaccurate. There was a dark side to HS that most wish neither to recall nor to convey. That dark side was the cruel treatment that I was accorded by certain members of HS. I am including examples of this treatment here, not because I wish to exact revenge, but because I wish to cleanse myself of the canker-like sores that have invaded my guts due to the resentment I have felt for over fifty years. If I forgive the ones who perpetrated these evils upon my body and soul, I will achieve a catharsis which will relieve me of these sores. Through this process I hope that my soul, like Dorian Gray's, will regain its beauty and goodness.

The First and Most Classic Forgiveness

A year after our Boston Latin School fiftieth reunion, we decided to hold our own little reunion in France. It would be organized by Arthur Bloom, who was residing in Paris with his wife, Deborah, and their son, Noah. Those in attendance were Billie and Don (Donnie) Orenbuch, Martha and Sumner (Zummy) Katz, Barbara and Jerome (Jerry) Davidow, Shae and Paul Rosenthal, Leila and Arnold (Arnie) Abelow, Cindy and Martin (Marty) Mintz, Julie and R. Arthur (Ray) Leiter and, of course, the Blooms (Archie). One of the events was a meeting of the AZA men modeled on the meetings we used to hold when we were active during our high school years. The first order of business was an attempt by the members to bring the group up to date on what had been going on in our lives in the past fifty years. I used the occasion to give birth to the forgiveness stories.

This episode took place at a "house date" with a BBG chapter. BBG, B'nai B'rith Girls, is the women's order of B'nai B'rith Youth Organization (BBYO), an international youth-led high school sorority for Jewish youth. It was considered a sister organization to AZA. A house date was a party arranged by the AZA and BBG chapters. The biggest prize that a guy could take from the party was a phone number or two. This particular house date took place at one of the girl's houses in Malden, just outside Boston. Transportation, in the form of automobiles, was at a premium. I was lucky enough to be offered a ride by one of the guys. Just how lucky you will see.

We arrived at about 8:00 p.m., eight to ten guys and the same number of girls. Liquor was not served at these gatherings, only snacks and soft drinks. Everybody attempted to make conversation. Things were pretty relaxed at this particular gathering; we weren't shy. The evening progressed at a rapid clip.

I happened to be looking out the window at about 11:30 when I heard a voice behind me saying, "Well, I think it's time to go now." It was the pater familias. I glanced around, looking for my friends, and, in particular, for my ride home. Not there. There was nobody left except Pater and the girl who lived there.

Pater said that all the guys and girls had left. I was incredulous. How was I to get home? My only choice was the subway. I would have to hurry because the system closed down at 1:00 a.m. and the journey, even in the rush hours, was at least an hour. At this time of night, it would take longer because of there being fewer trains and street cars running. Pater told me the direction to the nearest subway station, about half a mile. The son of a bitch did not offer me a ride.

It took over a long hour, after several transfers, to get to my final street car at Eggleston Square. I was sweating it because I could catch only the final run. If I missed it, I was plumb out of luck and faced a long, a very long, walk.

As I descended the stairs to the ground level, I saw the conductor about to signal the last car to pull out. I yelled, "Wait, wait!" He graciously held the car and I sprinted on board for the final twenty-minute ride to Wilcock Street, where I fell into bed, physically, emotionally, and psychologically drained.

To this day, I believe I was left on purpose because the others in my car had hooked up and didn't want me, who had not, to be a fifth wheel. Their raging hormones had overcome the usual "one for all, all for one" ethos.

And now, fifty years later at our reunion, I named the culprit. Do you know what he said?! He said, "I wasn't there." You don't believe me? I have it on videotape.

Nevertheless, to rid myself of this gnawing canker sore in my guts, I forgive you…

MARTIN M. MINTZ.

Marty's Rebuttal

Raymond…

I have a major grudge against you….

That evening at Honfleur, when Abelow and I did that hilarious take-off on Bloom, everyone laughed unto tears and you supposedly videotaped the evening….

151

All I ever saw was some footage of Donny, and scenes, blurred and nondescript, of the countryside from a moving car.

Then you told some lame story that you ran out of film and didn't know it??? How could that happen without your camera blinking lights at you!

So I can only conclude that you deliberately sabotaged the filming process so we have no record of that hilarious high point of the trip....

Shall I forgive this "oversight"?

Since Yom Kippur is just past, I can and will forgive you....

Ray.

Ray's Rebuttal to Marty

I never said I ran out of film. A camcorder does not run out of film. The battery went dead.

I am just as disappointed as you for not getting that uproarious performance.

Second Forgiveness: My First Drunk

During the summer of 1952, I prepared to enter college by developing a taste for beer. The opportunity presented itself because the rest of my family was away at the beach. By drinking just a little at a time, gradually increasing the dosage, I intended to become a full-fledged initiate into the joys of beer by the time of my Harvard orientation. The climax of this preparation occurred at an end-of-summer party at the home of Richard (Dick) Israel. It was a wild and crazy time and I became thoroughly smashed.

[Sidebar: On the way home (they didn't forget me this time), I remember stopping outside a drugstore in Grove Hall, as the neighborhood was called. Jerry Davidow and I had both worked there, I earning sixty cents per hour, but Jerry earning only fifty cents per hour. In this world, you get what you pay for.]

I was driven to my door, but one of my friends had to ring

152

the bell as I couldn't find my key nor would I have been able to use it had I found it. We were let in by the buzzer, but my friend ran away, leaving me dangerously to negotiate the stairs by myself. How I made it up I'll never know. I could have had a serious accident.

Nevertheless, I forgive you…
ARNOLD I. ABELOW.

Addendum: Arnie and I were roommates at Harvard during our senior year. He has much more for which to forgive me than I him.

Jerry's Rebuttal
Ha! By the summer of 1952, my family had moved to West Newton, and I worked at the Star Market in Wellesley, making eighty-five cents an hour! Plus, there were tips for carrying out shopping bags to the ladies' cars (this was Wellesley—women had cars.) Sometimes the tips added as much as thirty or forty cents to my day's wages.

In this world, you get what's coming to you.

I got the highly prized job at Shapiro's through some family pull. My father had a pharmacy on Blue Hill Avenue before he became a physician and he knew Jack from the old days.

Third Forgiveness: The Baseball Game
I was athletic. The problem was that my peers were not willing to acknowledge my baseball athleticism. What I lacked in speed, power, throwing strength and accuracy, and ability to make contact between bat and pitched ball, I more than made up for with my baseball smarts. I was scrappy. I knew where to shade the batter. Unlike Mo Vaughn, who played for the Red Sox, I could score from third on a triple. Nevertheless, the manager never let me into the game unless only nine men showed up. Which happened once.

I was assigned to play right field, except for left-handed batters, when I was told to exchange positions with the left fielder. I was given very explicit directions that, if by some miracle I should get my hands on the ball, I was to throw to the nearest man.

Now those of you who have ever played or watched baseball know that the most difficult ball for an outfielder to catch is a rising line drive hit directly at him.

To illustrate, note the following actual internet posting:[*]

"Fresno State Softball Win

Sophomore Robin Mackin threw a three-hitter and junior Michelle Palazuelos hit a two-run homer to lift Fresno State to a 3-1 victory over Connecticut on Tuesday in the first game of a doubleheader at Bulldog Diamond.

The Bulldogs took a 3-0 lead in the sixth with one out. Coronado doubled to the right-field gap and Palazuelos followed with a rising line drive to right. Outfielder Sarah Neuschwander misjudged the flight, ran in and the ball sailed over her head to the fence. Palazuelos, the team's fastest runner, came all the way around, beating the throw home by a couple steps."

So, naturally, the first ball hit to me was, as ordained by the sociopath who lives in the sky and has it in for me, a rising line drive, right at me. Like Sarah Neuschwander, I ran in and the ball sailed over my head. This did not endear me to my teammates.

Later, another batter lofted (as they say) an easy fly ball to right field, my position. I called for it quite clearly in my lirico-spinto tenor. Then, to my amazement, I heard the sound of a basso, the center fielder, also yelling "No, Ray, I got it." "No, it's mine." "Ray, get out of my way." "It's mine." And then the centerfielder did something to which even Alex Rodriguez wouldn't stoop. He shoved me out of the way with his shoulder

---

[*]Posted by Jeff Davis on March 6, 2007, 07:34 p.m.

and made the catch!

You cannot imagine my humiliation! What an ungracious act! But I would bide my time. Revenge would be sweet. I didn't have to wait long. The very next batter hit a ground ball just fair over the first-base bag with the ball coming to rest beside a man sitting on the grass in right-field foul territory watching the game. I picked up the ball and did exactly as I had been told.

I hadn't seen the centerfielder for fifty years until the 2006 AZA reunion. I had been suffering a sour stomach every time I thought about this incident. Nevertheless, for my own well-being and salvation, I state unequivocally that I forgive you....

MOE DRATCH.

View From the Other Side: Morrie's Rebuttal

This centerfielder—who patterned himself after Willie Mays—does not remember that event to which you refer. Perhaps I can reconstruct the event as it probably happened.

If the ball was hit directly at you (the right fielder), it would have been highly unlikely that I could have run from my position in centerfield to right field and caught that sphere.

Although I could catch a ball like Willie (I won't be modest about that), I was limited by my foot speed (otherwise slow).

What makes sense is that the ball was hit to rightcenter field. Both of us raced to catch the ball and shouted " I got it." At that time I did not hear you since your lyrical tenor voice had not reached its full strong maturity. Also, I was so focused on catching the ball, I zoned out all extraneous noises, including yours and the cheering spectators.

We have all seen collisions occur in baseball when two players are rushing to catch a ball despite both shouting, "I got it." I believe that is what happened to us. As you know, baseball is a game of inches. If you were a couple of inches closer to the ball, you would have made the catch.

You should not have felt humiliated since you made a gallant effort, and no forgiveness is required. If you want to publish your story, I would like this postscript version added.

Ray's Rebuttal to the Rebuttal
Willie Mays? I don't think so, Morrie; Cat Metkovich, maybe.

Fourth Forgiveness: A Different Sort of Baseball Game

…So we're walking together in the Harvard Yard, my friend and I, when I casually mention that, as treasurer of the Pierian Sodality (The Harvard-Radcliffe Orchestra), I have a key to a large room that is used as PS headquarters. I laughingly state that it would be pretty easy to sneak a girl in and make use of one of the two couches. For my friend, however, this is no laughing matter. He immediately suggests that we make use of this golden opportunity ASAP. "What, are ya kiddin'?" says I. "We get caught, we're outta here." He cajoles and cajoles; I resist. "We could be expelled!" "Tell ya what, I'll get y'a girl, too." "Sure," says I. He says that they will be sisters—not nun-type sisters but sister sisters—and that they are Catholic. I can hardly contain myself; this is a sure thing!

On the appointed night, we pick up the girls and drive them to Harvard. I unlock the PS door with much trepidation, hoping against hope that we're outta there before the scheduled rounds of the night watchman.

The couples go to separate couches (I had insisted on that) and start making out. Judging by the noise emanating from the other side of the room, my friend was rounding second, preparing to slide into third.

Meanwhile, I had scratched out a hit and was on first. It seemed as if, no matter how hard I tried, I was destined to be stranded there. My seduction skills were not as well honed as my friend's. Nevertheless, I keep trying…and trying…and trying. My stealing second, given my lack of speed and subtlety, is out of the question. But, as I mentioned above, I possess base-ball smarts. The strategy is obvious; I would bunt, thus sacrific-ing myself to second. It couldn't be easier.

I attempt to bunt on the first two pitches and miss both of them. Do I bunt with two strikes, thus making out if I hit a foul? There can be only one answer. I have nothing to lose by trying to bunt and second base to gain.

Jim Britt describes the action:

"The crowd is hysterical…Here's the windup…here's the pitch…Leiter lowers his bat…he gets wood on the ball…it's fair…right back to the pitcher…Parnell picks it up… throws to Doerr, getting Leiter at second…Doerr to Goodman…Leiter is also out at first. Ladies and gentlemen, I don't believe this. For the first time in baseball history, a batter has hit into a double play, doubling himself off at two different bases!"

Time to go home. My friend has his triple, sliding into third just as he was tagged (tie to runner). I don't begrudge him his triple. But wouldn't you think he would have made more of an effort to find me a less skilled defensive player? It was very selfish and mean-spirited on his part to think only of himself, when I was putting myself in danger of expulsion. What did he care? After all, it was I who had supplied the key and would be deemed the guilty party.

But it's water over the bridge…under the dam…whatever. There is no use in holding a grudge after fifty years—it just makes you sick. After all, Harvard can't rescind my diploma. Can they?

So I announce to all, I hereby forgive…

ARTHUR BLOOM.

And suggest the following tribute:

Arthur Bloom:

Great Doctor…..

Great Writer…..

Lousy Pimp!

Fifth Forgiveness: For the single most heinous mean-spirited rotten indescribable improbable foolish miserable ignorant foul hateful vomit-inducing cruel malevolent malicious nasty spiteful virulent scoundrelly obnoxious action ever taken against me.

I forgive you…

DON ORENBUCH.

Whoa! Wait just a minute!

The reader may ask:

1. Why are you giving us the name of the forgivee up front, and

2. How could a great guy like Don have done something so vile?

First, when I tell you this story, it will make more sense to know beforehand that the culprit was Don. Second, yes, Don is a great guy, so you will find this story all the more incredible.

In the early sixties, after I had moved to New York, I had the opportunity to be a member of the ensemble in Dorothy Raedler's American Savoyards, a Gilbert & Sullivan repertory company. We would perform off-Broadway at the Jan Hus Theater on the east side of Manhattan. However, the compensation would be extremely low and I would not be able to afford it. I had an idea. I asked Don if he would let me live in his apartment with him rent-free for the three months of the run. After that, I would look for another place. Don graciously agreed and I was very grateful.

It was a terrific summer; all I did was perform in the evening and hang around during the day. And I do mean hang around. I could not afford any outside entertainment so I did a lot of reading and TV watching.

Furthermore, I had to eat cheaply without sacrificing my health. One of my staples was chicken hearts, which not only were rich in protein, but also cost about thirty cents a pound. They were easy to sauté for about ten minutes with a little

Worcestershire sauce. I even made a dinner of chicken hearts for Don and served the leftovers the next night as cold chicken (heart) salad. With Don providing the wine, we had a gourmet meal fit for a king.

Like all good things, the summer and the run came to an end and it was time to look for my own place. But not too diligently. I struck a deal with Don that I would now pay half the rent until I moved out. I looked and I looked (yeah, right) but was unsuccessful.

Meanwhile, I had been dating a certain woman for quite a while. One evening she suggested that we blind double date, with Don dating her roommate. My girlfriend brought her roommate to the apartment and introduced me and Don to her. Her name was Billie. The rest, as they say, is history.

Meanwhile, I stayed on…and on…and on. Don would later refer to me as the man who came to dinner. Finally, what I had hoped would happen happened. Don married Billie and could not persuade her to move into the apartment. And no wonder. It consisted of one small bedroom, one small living room, and one tiny kitchen. Bathroom, of course. Therefore, Don and Billie moved to Queens and I inherited the apartment.

So you ask what was the problem; why do you have to forgive Don? Seems like he went out of his way to help you at great inconvenience to himself. And I don't deny that he did. But consider….

Do you remember what I said above? It was the sixties. Do you remember the sixties? Flower children, protests, summers of love, blah…blah…blah. But what was the real defining change of the sixties? Think about it. What was changing all over the country and perhaps most of all in New York? That's right. It was the SEXUAL REVOLUTION….

And Don never told me about it!

I could have been seriously injured.

Sixth Forgiveness: "Action"

Like the rest of red-blooded American youth, the AZA youth had raging hormones. One of the guys always wanted to visit a certain club because there was a lot of "action" there. Every time he could, he persuaded us to drive there. I was never that enthusiastic—you'll find out why later—but I would go anyway. The club was located in a seedy part of Boston, which later became famous as "the war zone." The entrance was difficult to spot if you did not know the location—there was no sign. To get in, one had to go down a long, steep, dark, narrow flight of stairs. Then you turned a corner, pulled open a heavy door, again with no sign. And voilà—"THE FRENCH VILLAGE."

They would set up a table and a provocatively clothed waitress would take our orders. We would commence our evening of ogling. I inquired of our provocateur as to when the action would begin. He told me to wait. I inquired of our provocateur as to when the action would begin. He told me to wait. I inquired of our provocateur as to when the action would begin. He told me to wait. Are you getting the idea? After an hour or so, we decided we'd had as much action as we could take.

As we were heading home, I realized what our provocateur had meant by action: getting high on ginger ale and looking at the waitresses. You should be ashamed.

Who should be ashamed? I'm not sure. I thought it was Mintz, but he denies it. Says he doesn't remember The French Village. Sounds like a Bloom thing but I don't think so. Rodman and Heifetz were probably involved. Abelow says it was a group project.

So I forgive you…
ANONYMOUS.

II. The Theater and Opera

This section is dedicated to the late Alice Schafer, Bob Shepley and Fran Walker. Alice, Bob and Fran were invaluable members of Somerset Valley Players (SVP) in Neshanic, New Jersey. I directed Alice in "Eastern Standard" and "Generations"; I directed Bob and Fran in "The Actor's Nightmare."

"Line up against the wall...by height," commanded the teach, the Boston Latin School drama club advisor. As always, I, a nice Jewish boy, did as I was commanded. I was the shortest and was, therefore, commanded to leave—too short. Thus ended my high school acting career. I joined the glee club instead and did not return to straight acting until we moved to New Jersey. I auditioned for and then joined SVP, where I made my debut as "Renfield" in *Dracula*. In community theater, I played character and singing roles in about fifteen shows. Among the most rewarding were Renfield in *Dracula* and Mr. Snow in *Carousel*.

During one of my terms on the SVP board, I was responsible for producing entertainment for the monthly meetings. I decided, on a lark, to direct a performance of *An Actor's Nightmare* by Christopher Durang. I enjoyed it a lot, the single performance was well received, and I discovered I had some talent for directing. SVP invited me to direct several productions.

Directing displaced singing and acting is my favorite theater activity. I am grateful to SVP for the opportunity.

The two qualities that helped me most in directing were my love of actors and the ability to cast well. Casting is the single most important thing a director does. Good actors can save a performance from a bad director, but a good director cannot save a performance from bad actors. I believe that I have made very good choices in my actors.

One choice was Bob Vaias, one of the best actors I have seen on any stage, professional or amateur. He played "Garfinkle" in

Other People's Money and "Mel" in *The Prisoner Of Second Avenue* and was brilliant in each role. His cooperation and kindness made work easy for all his colleagues.

Lona Alpert is a terrific character actor. She was in *Prisoner Of Second Avenue*. Her character appears in only one of the several scenes but was very memorable. I learned later that she had been offered a paying part for the run of our show but she elected to stay with us, since she had committed. We didn't pay a penny.

I hesitated to name the two actors above because I love and adore all the actors and crew I've ever directed.

I want to write about two other actors whom I did not direct but are the only two professional actors with whom I've ever had more than a fleeting relationship.

In 2001, my wife, Julie, and I visited Scotland, Great Britain, to take in the Edinburgh Fringe Festival, the largest arts festival in the world. Because there was a feast of 1,500 plays on offer, it was important to choose wisely to make the most of our time there. One show in particular caught our eye. This was *Sholom Aleichem—Now You're Talking!* a one-man show of the stories of Sholom Aleichem, adapted and performed by a South African-born, London-based actor, Saul Reichlin. The performance was extraordinarily impressive.

One lunchtime, at a sidewalk cafe in one of the teeming streets of Edinburgh, the actor Saul Reichlin walked by. We recognized him immediately and we got talking. I suggested that he join Julie and me for a bite to eat, and we soon became friends, in the way that followers of the work of Sholom Aleichem *(Fiddler on the Roof)* are likely to do. In the intervening years Saul has brought his show to many cities in the U.S., and he was a guest in our home in New Jersey. We are still corresponding between Arizona and London, and it is my hope that he will present his show here, when Julie and I will be able to renew our friendship with him and also acquaint our great state with the 100-year-old taste of "the old country."

Finally, I have been most fortunate to have met Alan Arkin and his wife, Suzanne, through attendance, five times, at his workshop dealing with self exploration through improvisation. My original motivation was to have fun and be in the aura of a famous and talented actor, one whose performances, beginning with *The Heart Is a Lonely Hunter*, I had always more than admired. The fun part was always fulfilled. More importantly, I got to know Alan and Suzanne a little through observation and conversation. Alan is a multi-talented man. He is a musician and a writer. He has written several children's books and an autobiography. The autobiography is concerned mostly with his relation to Buddhism. He is the co-composer of the Harry Belafonte hit "The Banana Boat Song" ("Tally Me Banana") and was a member of the folk group The Tarriers. He is a founding member of Second City. Suzanne, besides helping Alan in the classes, is a therapist. One of the joys of the classes was observing their marriage. My guess is that he is a spiritual man but not conventionally religious. I hope we meet again.

III. The Best Is Last: Julie

I have been blessed with a wonderful extended family of aunts, uncles, cousins and in-laws. My sister, Irma, is an extraordinary person to whom I am grateful for her taking care of our mother and brother. My niece, Lisa, is a spiritual person with much love to give. I have great in-laws.

In New York, I socialized with a group of amateur singers who met once a month at someone's apartment to read and sing a Gilbert and Sullivan operetta. On one occasion, I was cast as Richard Dauntless in *Ruddigore*. Julie Roterus was cast as Zorah the bridesmaid, who doesn't enter until toward the end of the show. Her few lines are a duet with Dauntless. They marry in the show and, some time later, in real life. Neither of us can believe it's been almost thirty years.

Julie has broadened my horizons in many ways.

First, she is an accomplished pianist and we have spent many an enjoyable hour doing songs and arias together. The highlight of this collaboration was a performance of Schubert's song cycle "Die schöne Müllerin," for our friends.

Second, she is a tennis enthusiast, got me into the sport, and beat me consistently. She also introduced me to horseback riding.

I am most grateful for her love of animals, which she has instilled in me. Growing up, I had not had animals. In fact, I was sometimes apprehensive in the presence of a dog. Our first animal was a turtle that Julie owned before we met. He is now over thirty-five years old and going strong. Julie took me and the turtle to a seminar on communicating with animals, and the turtle and I now have a beautiful relationship. He has the run of the house and likes to sit on my lap. Meffie is our beloved black cat, named for the opera character, Mefistofele. All our animals, except our horse, have been named after opera characters. The horse is named Seattle. He is a descendant of Seattle Slew and War Admiral. Because of Julie's shoulder problems and Seattle's hoof problems, Julie has not been able to ride him but she grooms him and brings treats almost every week.

She is kind, intelligent and beautiful.

I am a lucky man.

CHAPTER NINE

Jerry Sadow

M Y MOTHER CLUTCHED ME tight as the wind outside our first-floor bedroom in our tiny apartment in Nazing Court on Maple Street in Roxbury howled at 120 mph. But it was not the wind that scared us as it whipped against the three-story red brick building. It was the tree, a huge elm tree about thirty feet away, directly across an alley on higher ground, that swayed and groaned as it threatened to uproot and crash through the wall and windows. It did not fall in that history-making and extraordinarily destructive hurricane of September 1938 when I was four. But the situation—alone with my mother, with my father selling dresses on the road, fearful and crying, yet feeling protected by her that the worst would not happen—was to epitomize my emotions and my behavior in my early years.

In 1942, at the outset of World War II we rolled tinfoil into balls, first small then as large as baseballs. It was our contribution to the war effort. No one knew when we brought this prize to one of the stores on Humboldt Avenue whether it really was used and turned into bullets or armor, or dumped. But my parents did it as did most of the families who lived in Jewish

Roxbury. Conformity and unquestioning response was the norm. The immediate area was all low-rise apartment buildings, mostly red and brown brick, with a scattering of two-families and the occasional single-family house. In growing up, all of my friends lived in modest apartments, as did all of the families we knew, as well as my mother's married sisters and their children, my first cousins, who also lived in Roxbury. I didn't know any kid who lived in his own house or had his own bathroom.

To say that everyone lived in modest one-, two- or sometimes three-bedroom apartments does not accurately reflect my living conditions from birth until I went away to college at eighteen. Apartment #4 at 4 Nazing Court was less than 600 square feet for the three of us. You opened the door into the living room, about 10x14; straight ahead was the bathroom, about 5x8; to the right the kitchen, about 12x12; and to the left, through curtained French doors, the one bedroom, about 12x16. I was to sleep in that room with my parents, on a three-foot-wide cot with a silver metal structure on mostly a non-inner-spring mattress at the foot of their bed for eighteen years. That cot is in the basement of my house in Brookline.

We were poor but not so poor that my father, Bill, who of course in the 1930s, '40s and early '50s was the only one who worked, could not have moved us into a two-bedroom apartment for another $4 to $10 a month. But my mother, Sarah, nee Shapiro, who of course kept track of the money, paid the rent and the bills, was so, so scared that in any month in any year my father, working mostly on commission, would lose his job selling women's clothing, mostly as a traveling salesman, sometimes as an inside wholesaler, never owning his own business, that we never moved, even in a "good" year.

Strangely, I didn't feel raggedy poor, even though I was the only one I knew who slept in the same room with his mother and father, and knew that my friends thought it strange. The lack of space, with no place to sit and play, with not any area of privacy, was the main reason I rarely invited friends over. However, I don't remember once getting angry and screaming, "For God's sake, can we get a larger apartment!" although I'm sure I felt resentment. I accepted living this way because apparently I felt secure in the love of my parents for their only child, under their protection and watchfulness.

My mother was the main source of my sense of security. Paradoxically, Sarah had a lot of insecurities, not a confident personality, full of anxieties and fears, which manifestly or subliminally were reflected in my upbringing and behavior, and which led in part to cause difficulty with my peer relationships through puberty and even somewhat at the beginning of college. She grew up in the West End of Boston with four sisters, graduated from Girl's High, learned to play the piano, took salesgirl jobs in department stores before meeting and marrying my father in 1929 at the age of twenty-six. Playing the piano was a great joy to her, although not by any means a serious pianist, and when they visited friends she was always asked to play. Sadly and very unfortunately, for all of the twenty-two years she lived in the Roxbury apartment she denied herself buying even the smallest upright, whether for lack of space or presumed lack of money. That denial was part of her self-abnegation.

They lived with her parents, Russian immigrants who eloped in the 1890s as teenagers to escape the Czar's army, tramped across Europe, landing initially in Philadelphia before moving to Boston. Her relationship with two older sisters and one younger, growing up and also when they married into better economic circumstances living in Roxbury and then Brookline, was to define her personality: indecisive, deferring to her sisters on matters inconsequential and important. Their arguments, which were periodic but constant, evolved around the tiniest slight of word or action and rotated among the sisters so that two sisters would not speak to each other for weeks or months. What to buy, where to go, what to do in a given situation—bickering over "next to nothing" because they didn't have the emotional support of intellectual curiosity, hobbies, or outside interests. Only one sister worked part-time helping her husband in a candy business, so they had plenty of time to kvetch and kvell.

My father, born in Manchester, England, came to Plymouth, Massachusetts, at the age of two, grew up dirt poor with five brothers and a sister, never graduated from high school, and I never asked specifically how many grades he completed. I never wanted to embarrass Bill, especially since I was on an educated path to Boston Latin School. His father, my grandfather, was a peddler of dry goods on the streets of Plymouth and also an itinerant "rebbe" who went to the local jail to give solace and read blessings to Jewish prisoners. He was one of the original group who founded a schul in Plymouth. He died in his fifties before I was born. Other Sadow relatives were more prosperous, one owning the largest clothing store in Plymouth, aptly named SADOW'S.

Bill came to Boston when he was twenty or twenty-one, and found a job in the schmata business, where he would stay for the rest of his life, always working for others, who were small-time dress manufacturers or wholesalers, always mostly on the road taking heavy sample bags to retail stores in New England. Only once, for a few years, was he his own boss with a friend as a dress/blouse wholesaler in a small space at 75 Kneeland Street in Boston, the center of women's wholesale clothing for at least half a century, from the 1920s to the 1970s. His business failed within three years. During these times he was really close with only one brother, older, who had a small trucking business in this garment district. He met and visited with other brothers and his sister, who lived either in Massachusetts or Rhode Island, usually on family markings of birthdays, anniversaries and Bar Mitzvahs.

Bill had a prickly personality, uneducated, quick to lose his temper and quick to fight if provoked, although small and wiry. I grew up sometimes afraid of him, although the times he hit me were few, and he extended his love and care for me as much as he could emotionally, especially when it came to sports. There I am at the age of about five, dressed in a baseball outfit, or playing catch with him, or listening to the Red Sox and Bruins games on radio together at home. And he was at home for the most part, but his selling travels frequently meant he was away for a night or two every few weeks. He did not provide the overwhelming love and care and caution of Sarah, but on balance he was a pretty good father, protecting me when I got into scrapes with an unfriendly kid, scrapes that I usually lost. But the emotional bond was only sports. We talked little about school or politics or Jewishness, areas where he had little learning and was reluctant to speak for fear of showing his ignorance.

In a Roxbury area bounded by the major streets of Seaver Street and Franklin Park on one side and Blue Hill Avenue and Grove Hall stores on the other, my immediate neighborhood of Nazing Court and Maple Street included residential streets named Sonoma, Wayne, Nazing, Hutchings, and Homestead, and major avenues named Humboldt and Elm Hill, where at the corner with Seaver, was located Temple Mishkan Tefila and its Hebrew school, where I studied for five grades. Mishkan Tefila was the absolute heart and center of Conservative Judaism in Roxbury, a very large column-fronted building with Greek, Gothic and Romanesque architectural elements that brought together in its 1,000-plus family-membership religious and religiously knowledgeable Jews, and Jews who knew no Hebrew, could not follow the religious service and did not attend—Jews only by culture, tradition and conforming pressure.

So this neighborhood was virtually all Jewish, an undefined ghetto without borders, freely moved into and held together by the necessary feelings of security and safety. It was strictly middle class in the sense that hardly any men, the only gender working in those decades, were blue-collar factory workers, or on the other hand white-collar corporate/business executives. What the fathers were, in what were for the most part stable two-parent families, were independents that carved out income neither by having to report to goyish or Jewish bosses nor by working in assembly line jobs. My father and the fathers of most of my friends were clothing salesmen, tradesmen, owners of small hardware stores, tobacco and convenience stores, insurance reps, jewelry wholesalers. They were middlemen in the economy, in positions that allowed some independence and control of their jobs and finances. Rarely were these fathers professionals on a career track—not lawyers, doctors, academics, engineers, scientists. Hardly any of them had gone to college, except for the occasional dentist.

It was with the children of these families, like mine, lower-income but not feeling poor because virtually everyone in the neighborhood lived in the same financial circumstance, that I went to the William Lloyd Garrison Elementary School for seven years, from kindergarten through sixth grade. Garrison was the outraged, passionate and absolutist anti-slavery abolitionist who is historically famous for publishing *The Liberator* in the 1830s. The school architecturally was a semi-horseshoe, red-brick building from three to five stories. The boys and girls at the Garrison were mostly Jewish, while the teachers were all single Catholic women—single because the Boston school system didn't want to hire engaged or married women who would get pregnant and have to leave their classes during the school year, then leave the system to take care of their babies. This was a secure and happy time for me, with lots of boy friends from the neighborhood and the school, where I did very well in my school subjects and played stickball and boxball (hit a bouncy rubber ball with your fist and try to get it in between or by the four infielders on the asphalt surface).

The dichotomy in my "getting along" with my peers probably started when I was ten or eleven, in the fifth grade, just before the onset of puberty, when I had good friendships with kids in groups and then clubs, but individually was outspoken, overly candid in expressing opinions, sometimes negative, cynical and downright insulting or defensive, not realizing I was not diplomatic or compromising in order to maintain good relationships. I developed a "big mouth," saying harsh truths that some boys didn't want to accept or hear or admit to. One can psychoanalyze this persona endlessly: overprotected, always getting my way at home, physically small and not good at fighting back, "the nature of the beast," genes, strong feelings of personal injustice, pride, temper. This personal dichotomy, accepted into boys clubs, good at sports, strong intellectually on one hand; verbally too truthful, sometimes unaware I was hurting feelings, withdrawing on occasion into loner behavior on the other, was to stay with me through puberty, high school and the beginning of college, until about the age of twenty. It was to cause many emotionally painful moments.

I was accepted into the Boston Latin School in the seventh grade and was there for six years, until graduation, like a number of my boy friends from Roxbury and then from the Haym Salomon AZA. Academically, I started out very well, coping with the discipline, three-hour-a-night homework, sometimes strange and unfriendly teachers who often were frustrated PhDs teaching in a high school, although a high school in the forties and fifties that was nationally recognized, attracted paying students from outside of Boston, had one hundred percent of the seniors admitted to good four-year colleges, and was one of the best public schools in the U.S.—as good as the best private schools of Exeter, Andover and their ilk. Outside of school during this time, from the sixth to the ninth grade, from age twelve to fifteen, I was a member of the Pythons, a boys sports club that met at the YMHA located at the corner of Seaver

Street and Humboldt Avenue in Roxbury. We had stunning black-and-red jerseys with numbers on the back, played baseball, football, bowling, occasional basketball and hockey, and tried in our chaotic club meetings at the "Y" as teenagers to occasionally make rational adult decisions.

Whether it was the impossibility of studying in a tiny apartment where the kitchen table/desk was only about ten feet away from the radio, or the teenage hormonal changes, or the by now infrequent individual boy-to-boy hostility, or because I was not as bright as thought, I did not do well in many of my classes at Latin School from the tenth to twelfth grade, and ultimately graduated by academic number near the bottom of the class of just under 200. I could say that I was academically deprived at home but I will never in all sincerity use that as an excuse or explanation. There wasn't a book in our apartment except for a dictionary and a Bible, maybe some *Reader's Digests* and a few novels by undistinguished authors. I don't remember seeing even children's books, although I'm sure my mother read to me. My parents never went to the library or read, and could not afford, or never thought to take me to, the theater or to a concert.

They certainly couldn't help me with Latin School homework. I spent many days and hours after school for several years studying in the Great Hall of the Boston Public Library, in an elevating but distracting environment. Just as well. In this period when my mother and father were in their late forties to early fifties, there were frequent arguments over money, the fear of moving to a higher-rent apartment, sister-to-sister flare-ups, and the usual at-home squabbling. Their sex life was probably nil, and not only because I slept in the same bedroom with them. I'm sure my father had affairs on his salesman travels, and this suspicion, sometimes fed by one or another of my mother's sisters, led to a tense atmosphere. Once, burned in my memory, whether the argument was over sex or money, Bill cornered Sarah at the bedroom closet and punched her to the floor. Scared and crying, along with my mother, I tried to hold him back. He stopped before any serious injury. Again, over the years my father hit me only a few times.

It was at this time, when I was sixteen and seventeen, in some difficulty at Latin School, in a fairly good relationship with Bill and Sarah, with home talk mostly about the dress business, sports, occasionally national and state politics, going to movies, and the eventual breaking up of the sports club Pythons, that I was accepted and voted into Haym Salomon AZA, not without some controversy and dispute in the voting, if I remember correctly. For me, it was a fortunate, fortuitous and very maturing event and experience. I knew many of this AZA's members from Latin School or from sports team contacts. But the group did include Jewish teenage aliens from Dorchester and Mattapan—I was, after all, from Roxbury. Joining the AZA provided a major transition from teenager to adult for me. The AZA in its cultural Jewishness was not about school or sports or personal relations or individual achievement. In its purpose for the twenty or so AZAers, helped by a few old men in their twenties, the discussions centered not on us but on the community and society, Jewish and Gentile. What can we do to improve social conditions? What charities can we contribute to, carry out *tsadaka*? How can we help elderly or sick people with visits and/or transportation? What Jewish wise men can we invite to talk about issues of the day? Which fundraising drive for some disease or health concern should we support and work for? What teenage activities, such as an organized dance, can we not only organize and attend and contribute to, but also hold to benefit some larger cause?

This approach was a revelation to me, perhaps not as mature in outlook as some of my friends, having a teenage club dealing with adult matters, furthering our Jewish knowledge but also exemplifying through Haym Salomon AZA the responsibility and obligation we as future Jewish adults have and must engage in. Think of others less fortunate. Join and contribute to your neighborhood, your community, your society, the essence of Judaism from biblical to current times. Be a mensch. And that is what I hoped to become, and derive from the AZA experience, from the really wonderful guys I sat next to, laughed with, and debated serious matters with at each meeting before ending with a unifying song.

At Latin School, besides the demanding courses in English, history, French, German, Latin, chemistry, physics, et al., joining the chess club, the literary, modern history, and French clubs, contributing to the school publication *The Register,* I played varsity tennis for three years and had the second highest bowling average in the school—that's candlepin bowling, with the small balls. I mention this because tennis was to give me pleasure and pain at the University of Massachusetts-Amherst when I started playing varsity tennis in my sophomore year and promptly flunked out of school due to a combination of tennis commitments, disinterest in certain mandatory courses, and not attending enough classes in two courses. Imagine—flunked out for non-attendance in the fifties and given no chance to stay at UMass, to take make-up courses in the summer, or to repeat a few courses in the fall semester.

I was admitted to UMass after only one honor in the college boards and very average SATs, with the help of the famous Latin School student college advisor, Lee J. Dunn, who called up the UMass admissions officer and said demandingly, "Jerry Sadow wants to go there. He deserves it, he'll be a good student, what do you say?" UMass was the best choice for my parents and for me; the total financial package came to only about $1,000 a year, and I finally left the by now embarrassing home sleeping arrangement for college and a small, shared dorm room with barebones amenities, a bed and a desk for each, and one wooden sitting chair.

In search for what I considered and wanted to be the most important, the most meaningful, the most personally satisfying things for my life, I majored in English literature, without regard for any future financial or career consideration. After flunking out, I went to summer school at Boston University, took two literature courses, came back to UMass as a junior taking a first semester of seven courses, including phys ed and some other gut requirement, and graduated within the normal four years, in 1956. I took the most demanding lit courses, mostly American and British, with a minor in philosophy, averaging B's in those two years.

What to do? Continue to be impractical, of course. I was admitted to the New York University graduate school with a small scholarship, majored in literature, minored in philosophy, lived in Greenwich Village for two years in quasi-bohemian fashion. My parents, especially my father, didn't know what the hell I was doing or what I wanted to do. When it came to a career, neither did I, since my attempts at "creative writing" were not successful and I didn't want to become an academic and teach. My mind was made up for me when, after dodging military service for as long as possible, I was drafted into the U.S. Army at the end of 1957, swinging unbelievably from the culture of Greenwich Village to basic training, as a private first class at Fort Benning, Georgia. I spent most of my military time overseas in Bamberg, Germany, where in addition to practicing war games in dreadful and muddy training spots, I wrote for military newspapers about my unit, Third Armored Division, Seventh Cavalry, 2nd Reconnaissance, and became a unit photographer after buying a Rolleiflex. Near the end of my two years as an enlisted GI, a choice made perhaps foolishly to escape serving four years but as an officer, I received notice from NYU that I didn't have to complete my master's thesis, which was to be on John Dos Passos, because I and so many others in the military had completed all courses and all other requirements. Thus I now had an M.A. in literature.

Trying to become practical, while still in Germany in the army, I applied to several graduate journalism schools, and was amazed and stunned when I was accepted to the Columbia Journalism School in New York City, the best journalism school in the country. I had prepped for Columbia's writing and current events test, given to me in Frankfurt, by reading *Time* and *Newsweek*. With no real journalism experience, I entered a select class of eighty-three in 1960 at the "J" School, intimidated not only by being tossed from the army to Columbia and its very demanding profs, but also by a number of students who had already worked as newspaper reporters or for other media. I lived near Columbia, at Broadway and 112th, again had a small scholarship, worked part-time, including being a gofer at *The New York Times,* and went to school as one would a job—nine to five, six days a week, from September to June—and received an M.S. degree in one year of Columbia's intense and concentrated program.

If I had thought my living conditions would really improve with more personal space when I left home for the first time, I was wrong. In New York, while at NYU, I lived in a small Greenwich Village room with kitchen and bathroom privileges; in the army I shared a barracks with forty to a floor at Fort Benning, then with about twelve to a room in Bamberg. While at Columbia in New York, I again rented what I could afford— a room with kitchen and bathroom privileges. This spatial confinement—I was now twenty-six—was to make privacy and space a priority for me for nearly the next fifty years.

After leaving the "J" School, I was to embark on a career, unplanned and mostly random, in journalism, government and politics, and public affairs. My first job was as a reporter for the *Boston Globe* for a year, then as a news editor at WBZ-TV in Boston for another year. I was then hired as press secretary to Edward W. Brooke, who was running for state attorney general as a Republican in 1962. He won and I won that November, and three weeks later I married Catherine Cuttler from Montreal at Temple Reyim in Newton, taking a three-day honeymoon in Nantucket.

I was to serve, starting at age twenty-eight, as press secretary to the Attorney General of Massachusetts, Edward Brooke, the first African-American elected to statewide office in the U.S. since Reconstruction, in the 1870s. For the next four years, I wrote hundreds of press releases, a number of speeches, and served as spokesperson dealing and meeting with the media, setting up press conferences for Brooke, and participating in his successful reelection run for AG in 1964. I went to the Republican National Convention in 1964 in San Francisco with Brooke and one other aide, wrote a short speech for him praising General and former President Dwight D. Eisenhower at a convention, at which he delivered a longer speech, nominating Senator Barry Goldwater for President.

In 1966 Brooke beat his rivals to the punch in deciding to run for the U.S. Senate and he won. After working hard in the Senate campaign I went with him to Washington, D.C., and Capitol Hill as his Senate press secretary at age thirty-three. Being introduced to and meeting Vice President Hubert H. Humphrey on the Capitol steps on my third official day in the Senate office in 1967 epitomized whom I met and talked to on many occasions in my two years in Washington—senators and their staff members, nationally known media columnists, reporters, and TV personalities. Funny. I remember having to rub knees with the wife of then Senator Howard Baker of Tennessee in the House of Representatives gallery at President Lyndon Baines Johnson's 1968 State of the Union speech.

By the end of 1968, I made a fateful decision that was to limit and perhaps downgrade my government public affairs career but enhance my quality of life and determine the lives of my wife and two sons. With my relationship with Senator

Brooke fraying after seven years with him, I decided not to take another Capitol Hill position and not to move from our northwest Washington apartment to a house in the Virginia or Maryland suburbs. With Catherine and not-yet-one-year-old first son, Jonathan, and having just had a house built in Wellfleet on Cape Cod, the first thing I ever owned, I moved back to a large but cheap rental apartment in Brookline and took a position as press secretary to the commissioner of the newly formed Massachusetts Department of Community Affairs. Building that house, a modern-looking, red-cedar-and-glass slider-door structure, was the smartest quality of life move I made, after marrying Catherine. In 1970, my second son, Joshua, was born in Boston.

Things soured quickly at that state agency. The state legislature didn't follow through with the promised funding of its new programs; the commissioner, also African-American, suddenly died of a heart attack; the new commissioner was antagonistic, and at the point of being fired, I used Senator Brooke's political clout to help me land the position in Boston of public affairs director for the New England regional office of the U.S. Department of Housing and Urban Development (HUD). I stayed in that position from 1971 to 1978, putting out information on the agency's housing, planning and urban development programs, and handling all press inquiries. On my own, this time, in 1978 I won the job as public affairs specialist at the U.S. Department of Transportation's (DOT) transportation systems center, a Cambridge-based national research facility for all of the major agencies of DOT—Federal Aviation Administration (FAA), U.S. Coast Guard (then part of DOT), National Highway Safety Transportation Administration (NHSTA), Federal Highway Administration (FHWA), Federal Railroad Administration (FRA). We also did research for the transportation secretary's office.

Catherine, a public school teacher first in Montreal, then

after marriage in Quincy, Massachusetts, got a master's in education from Boston University, and while the boys were in preschool, taught English as a Second Language (ESL) to adult immigrants at Brookline High School. She was to develop into a well-respected ESL teacher and authority, teaching for twenty-four years at Northeastern University's English Language Center, starting in 1980, coauthoring five ESL textbooks, and speaking at and delivering ESL papers at the annual national conferences of TESOL, Teachers of English to Speakers of Other Languages. With her added salary, I bought a house in Brookline in 1982, at the end of the Carter Administration, at the height of high interest but lower housing prices. Catherine is now teaching ESL at SHOWA at the Boston campus of this Japanese Institute for Women.

I was to stay as public affairs specialist at DOT's Transportation Systems Center, dealing with the media, writing press releases, helping to put out descriptive brochures and annual reports, for most of my eighteen years there, through 1996. I took a buyout then, at a time of DOT managerial upheaval, diminishing funding of programs and the constant threat of the wiping out of many civil service positions. For health reasons, since I have always been emotionally intense, it also was the right time—two years after my second heart attack, followed by bypass surgery. A few years later I started teaching as an adjunct professor, or part-time, at Boston University's College of Communication, teaching public relations, media relations and government public affairs courses in graduate and senior level classes, which continues to this day.

My sons, Jonathan and Joshua, graduated from Brookline High School. Jonathan majored in literature at Hampshire College in Amherst, Massachusetts, and Joshua in philosophy at Earlham College in Richmond, Indiana. Jonathan got a PhD in Comparative Literature at UMass-Amherst, married and divorced, taught literature in non-tenure positions at colleges in Massachusetts and Montreal, and in September 2008 [as of this writing] will start a tenure-track position teaching literature at the State University of New York's (SUNY) Oneonta campus. He will soon marry a woman from Montreal whom he met while teaching there at Concordia University. Joshua moved to Seattle to marry a childhood friend first met during summers in Wellfleet, got two master's degrees at the University of Washington, in public administration and Middle East studies, works at a county public administration job, and has two sons with his wife Nicole: Eli, soon to be seven; and Zachary, just turned four.

And me? Until compelled to write this narrative, I had not focused on the two years in Haym Salomon AZA, its purpose, its activities, its friendships, as a transitional force probably unacknowledged in expanding meaningful thought and behavior toward adulthood. The problems I had before this experience, whether by living conditions, my own behavior, parental behavior, peer circumstance, or other not fully defined reasons, have for the most part dissipated in the decades of marriage, media and public affairs comparative successes, children, friendships retained since the age of six, and newly formed individually, in organizations such as Temple Sinai in Brookline, where for several years I was a board of trustees member, and in the compromise and diplomacy of adult relations.

Oh yes, progress. My parents finally moved in 1957, when Roxbury was well into "turning" from Jewish to Negro, to a small two-bedroom apartment in Brookline. As soon as I could afford it, with my first job at the *Boston Globe*, I bought my mother a piano. In my life, I had moved from two rooms to two houses.

CHAPTER TEN

Don Orenbuch

I GOT THE CALL IN December 1961. Ma had died. There were plenty of flights from Manhattan to Boston and I arrived on the same day. It was this event that was to begin my interest in genealogy, family history, and family stories.

During the time that we sat shiva, many people came to that apartment on Astoria Street. I realized that while I knew some of these strangers by name, I knew little about how they were related to my mother, and of course to me. For reasons perhaps to be revealed later, we had not had much contact with the large Gorman family that had settled in Boston in the years before and after World War I. I grabbed some paper and sat at the mahogany dining room table and began to draw a family tree with my mother at the center.

I drew a little box, Ruth Orenbuch 1898-1961. Below that, another box with a thin line leading to it, Donald Orenbuch 1934-. The strangers clustered around me and told me where to put the next box. Uncle Meyer, Aunt Mae, Cousin Paula, all appeared in their crudely drawn box. The number of boxes grew. I soon had a spiderweb of lines, but Ma was no longer at the center. I never realized until many years later, how appropriate that was. With her death, she was no longer at the center of my life.

Over the week, as strangers came and went, I filled in more boxes. The number of sheets of paper grew, and my mother and I were pushed further from the center of the tree. Over the years, as the family tree grew, I taped these pages together, two, three, four. The papers came with me to family Bar Mitzvahs, weddings, Passover seders, and funerals. At first they were folded in the pocket of my jacket. But later, as the number of lines grew, the pages were in a large manila envelope.

I would pull people aside and asked them if they knew who married whom; what the parents' names were; when and where they were they born; when they died. The answers were rarely straightforward. There were often stories, great stories about the family. Often disputes arose as to how many children this or that cousin had and who was born first, who was second, who married whom. And, slowly the manila envelope became thicker.

What does all of this have to do with AZA? For a long time I have wanted to write a letter to my two children to describe what it was like to grow up in the Jewish ghetto of Boston, to live in the middle third of the twentieth century, and to write down just a few of the family stories. There is nothing new here. They both have heard these stories many times. When I start to talk about those early years, I see their eyes roll and I hear the thought go through their heads, here goes Dad again!

Here I can fulfill that need to describe a family's life in Jewish Boston. (I regret that when I heard the stories, I did not take a lot of notes. I was more focused on genealogy than family history.) At the same time I can fulfill my obligation to write a chapter for this book. Here goes Dad again.

Even before I can begin this letter, I have to explain to others who may be foolish enough to spend time reading this just who are the recipients of this letter, Tim and Evelyn.

Ten months after Billie and I were married, Joseph William Orenbuch was born, August 24, 1966. Less than two years later, we added another member to the family, Laura Ruth Orenbuch, June 8 1968. Joseph was named after my brother who died in World War II (more about him later). The Ruth in my daughter's name came from my mother. In both cases the names were really an Anglicization of Yiddish names, Yossie and Rivkah. We were now the ideal American family...one father, one mother, one boy, one girl, one dog, one cat.

We now have to abruptly jump ahead to 1977. I was employed by Anaconda, a mining and manufacturing company headquartered in Manhattan. The company had been acquired late in 1976 by ARCO, a petroleum company. I was asked if I wanted to move to Los Angeles to work in ARCO's headquarters to help educate the ARCO executives about the company they had just spent billions to acquire.

I was a "modern" married man and well versed in the necessity to involve family members in heavy decisions. I asked if I could think about the offer. That evening I told my family about the offer and asked if they would like to move from East Windsor, New Jersey, to Los Angeles. We had lived in a development, which had grown up in a field surrounded by farms not too far from Princeton, for eight years. It was the only home that the children could remember. Everyone—Billie, Joseph and Laura—were enthusiastic about the opportunity to move to California, where the sun never left the sky, and filled with movie stars and excitement.

I accepted the offer. I then met with Joseph and Laura (eleven and nine, respectively) and told them that they were moving almost three thousand miles away, to another coast, where no one knew them. It was a chance to change their young lives. They could change anything about themselves that they did not like. We were going to emulate those earlier settlers who in the 1860s and 1870s had given up their lives in the East for the wealth and a new start in the West.

Obviously, what I was thinking about was improving their school homework, being nicer to each other, keeping their rooms clean, etc. Joseph and Laura thought that it was a great idea and said that they would give some real thought to changes.

A couple of days later, they came to me and said that they both had decided to change something. They wanted to change their names! Laura Ruth Orenbuch wanted to become Evelyn Orenbuch; Joseph William Orenbuch wanted to become Timothy Patrick Livingston. "Joseph is such a common name," I was told. "I want to be named after my great-grandmother," said Laura.

In retrospect, I am surprised at how easily I took the request. I considered the request unusual but not unreasonable. What's the first thing you say to anyone whom you meet for the first time? "Hello, my name is_____." If your name is the first thing most people learn about you, why shouldn't you be allowed to pick your own name? In that sense it is not unreasonable. After all, I realized that I had changed my name. Few people called me Donald. To everyone I was Don.

Billie and I agreed! When we moved to L.A., in June 1977, Laura became Evelyn Laura Ruth Orenbuch. However, I put my foot down concerning Joseph's desire to change his last name. He became Timothy Joseph William Orenbuch. When we moved to California, they only responded to their new names. If we called out Joseph or Laura, we were ignored. I made a special point of warning the school system that they would be receiving records from East Coast schools for Joseph and Laura, but their real names were Tim and Evelyn. The names stuck.

That first year, I was briefly tempted to claim four dependents on my tax return. After all, I had records for four children:

Joseph, Tim, Laura and Evelyn. I resisted.

No, it's not the end of the story. Two years later, I was offered an opportunity to go back to the East Coast, Philadelphia, to work at ARCO Chemical Co. What to do about the names? We would be moving close to the area where we had lived. My East Coast relatives had all thought I was crazy to give in to the name change request. It was just a lot of mishigas.

I asked the children, now eleven and thirteen, what they wanted to do. Tim wanted to keep his new name. Evelyn had a more unique solution: east of the Mississippi she would be Laura, and Evelyn west of that divide. She was forced to choose, and she chose her new name. Since then, they have been known as Tim and Evelyn by all of their friends. Most do not know their real names.

Many years later, I asked why they had decided to keep their new names. I was told that the real reason was that it had taken a long time to train Billie and me to call them by their new names. They did not want to go through that again to have to train us to call them by their other names.

The Letter

Dear Tim and Evelyn,

I have never been a very spiritual person. In college I studied chemistry; in graduate school, business. The study of both of those leaves little room for thoughts of the spirit. Yet I have always believed that in me there is something more than just me. I feel a connection to all those who came before me. Although I never met my grandparents, and know little of them, I feel their presence in me.

I believe that part of this feeling stems from the Passover seder. Each year, my father would go through most of the seder and I would have to ask the four questions, both in Hebrew and in Yiddish. It was an unbreakable family tradition. As you know, in that seder we thank God for taking us out of bondage in Egypt. We do not give thanks for releasing the Jews: rather he released us. There seems to be a belief in a union of the past and the present and thus, perhaps, the future. Time is meaningless in the Jewish context. We are as one with those of the past. I believe this.

In the old country, as we seem always to refer to the place where we lived before the U.S., in the Jewish culture of the time, a man in his sixties needs a wife. In 1887, Litman Abba Orenbuch's first wife died. So, at the age of sixty-six, in the town of Konskie, Poland, in September 1888, with the aid of a matchmaker, he married. His bride, your great-grandmother, was Wita Rojza Dluznieswka, twenty-five years old. He must have been a pretty virile man because one year later, at the age of sixty-seven, in December 1889, Wita gave birth to Motel Orenbuch, my father, your grandfather. In another year, another child, Ida. And yet another, Jacob, who died after just a few days.

(As an aside, in case you ever want to do further research, be aware that in Polish the endings of last names will vary depending on whether it is a man or a woman. Hence Wita Dluzniewska's father was Dluzniewski. Just another thing that helps to make genealogy a real fun and difficult search process.)

The marriage certificate describes Litman as the son of Lea and Leiser Altman, and a landowner, having fulfilled his military service. That is pretty much all we know of him, because he died four years later, in 1893. Motel thus never really knew his father. He had a vague recollection of visiting some of Litman's relatives in the town, but in my search of the town's records I could not find any connections. Of course, if the relatives were married women, they would be listed under their husband's names. Only by going through thousands of town records, some in almost unreadable Polish script and others in Russian, looking for the maiden names of the brides, would I possibly be

DON ORENBUCH

able to find the connections. This was a process I have chosen
not to undertake.

Now, Wita was in the same situation that Litman had been
earlier. A young woman, alone, with two young children. As
before, a matchmaker was obtained. She arranged to have Wita
marry Mordechai Zeidman, the town baker. When we visited
Poland in 2005, we believe we found the site of his bakery. The
structure on the site was quite old and may have been the actual
building of the bakery. Another excitement of genealogy: to
be in an ancient site related to your family's history. The body
experiences an unusual sense of connection with the past.

According to Pa, he treated them all equally. Mordechai
was obviously an ambitious man. About 1900 he gave up the
relative security of the small town and moved to Lodz, ninety
kilometers away. Lodz was a large industrial town, needing a
good baker. It must have needed a good Jewish baker because
the family spoke Polish poorly. With a large Jewish population,
estimated to be as much as ten to fifteen percent of the entire
country, and whole towns made up of Jews, it was possible to
live in Poland and speak only Yiddish. When your grandfather
came to the U.S., and for all the years I knew him, he spoke
Yiddish, English (or Yenglish) and no Polish! He claimed to
know no Polish even though he had lived in that country for
about twenty-five years!

The entire family worked in the bakery. Motel learned his
trade from his father and became an excellent baker. I can attest
to that. He was a thin, tall man, pitch-black hair and strong
arms. I guess the strength came from years of hand-kneading
dough. His thinness came from years of working in the bakery, heavy with the heat and residue given off by charcoal-fired
brick ovens.

Now in order to go on from here, I need to tell you a bit
about Polish history. You see, even though I keep referring to

Poland, there was no Poland. Poland as a country had been conquered in 1798. The country had been divided into three parts: one given to the Austro-Hungarian Empire; one part to Germany; and one part to Russia. Lodz was in the Russian section. With war with Germany on the horizon, Russia needed troops to defend itself against the Huns. The Czar reached into the Polish section of his empire to conscript troops. He reached into Lodz. He touched Motel.

There was a provision in the conscription law that a conscript could hire someone to take his place in the army. (If that sounds strange, be aware that the U.S. had the same provision in its laws during the Civil War.) Mordechai hired someone, at considerable expense, to take Motel's place. But at the last moment that person reneged, and apparently disappeared with the money. At age twenty-three, Motel had to go into the Russian army.

Another of my core beliefs is that history repeats itself. Jews in Poland (Russia) were not quite full citizens, suffering under discriminatory laws. Yet they were good enough to be cannon fodder in a war. Sound familiar? Think about the U.S. experience in World War II, where we kept Negroes (as they were called at the time, or African-Americans now) in separate units…good enough to fight but not good enough to enjoy the rights of full citizenship because of Jim Crow laws.

Pa had to get out of Poland. One hallmark of a dictatorship, as Russia was, is that citizens need permission to do anything. Permission was needed to simply go from one town to another. Citizens went to the local police station and requested "papers" that would allow the trip. (Remember that the whole movie *Casablanca* is about "letters of transit" that allow the bearers to leave the country!) Pa could not get the papers, since the police were aware that he was due to be inducted into the army.

Motel fled the country under a pile of hay. In late 1911 or

early 1912, the hay wagon crossed the border into Austria. Pa was free of the Russian Czar.

Vienna became home for a few months. Pa had trouble with the nation's language, but there were enough Jews so that he could get by just speaking Yiddish. (It was said at that time that a person could travel the world by speaking only English or Yiddish.) He became a baker and began to save his money. His favorite memory was seeing Emperor Ferdinand in a carriage on the main street. Pa was impressed with his military bearing, his uniform and his great mustache.

In July 1912, from the port of Bremen, Motel left Europe and headed for Philadelphia. He left everything behind, his family, his friends, and his few possessions. Except for two family members, he never saw any of his family again. According to the ship's manifest, he had $18 in his pocket. I have always loved my father, your grandfather, and always had enormous admiration for him. Think about it. He moved to a new country, a new culture, not being able to read or speak the language, with just $18 and hope mixed with, I would expect, fear. I wonder who among us could do that.

In August 1912, Morris Orenbuch arrived in Philadelphia. Yes, he changed his name too!

We cannot appreciate where we are until we understand where we have been. So this story, for you, Tim and Evelyn, is to let you know my life, so as to perhaps better understand your father. So here goes Dad again. This is likely to be a stream-of-consciousness writing style.

Until five years old I lived in the middle of what I call the Jewish ghetto of Boston. It was a concrete apartment house at 108 Intervale Street. We lived on the second floor in what was called a "railroad" style of apartment, meaning that there was a long corridor that ran the length of the building and all of the rooms opened onto this corridor. There were six of us in an apartment that only had a couple of bedrooms. I really do not remember what the sleeping arrangements were, but they were obviously quite cramped. Since Pa, your grandfather, was a baker, he worked nights. So someone must have used his bed during the night and he used it during the day.

The six were Ma (Rivka, or Ruth, b. 1899) and Pa (Motel, or Morris, b. 1889), your Aunt Helen (b. 1918), Uncle Lou (b. 1920), Uncle Joseph (b. 1923) and me (b. 1934). (If I get time I will tell you how Ma and Pa met. They came from Poland individually and met in Boston. And it's another good family story.)

In the basement of this house was a small room. You entered this room by going down a few stairs from street level. An old man with a long beard, and always with a hat on, was trying to eke out a living from selling candy and a few canned goods. For real shopping we walked down to the end of Intervale Street where it connected with Blue Hill Avenue, one of the major streets through the ghetto. Streetcars ran along a median strip on this avenue. In the 1930s you could ride the cars for a few pennies.

Again, for someone who was raised in the suburbs, each with his own room and being driven everywhere to go shopping, this must be hard to imagine. Going shopping meant going to your favorite meat store, where the owner knew all his customers by name. Then off to the fish store, with the varieties stretched out on shaved ice. And so on. The only time I have seen this since my childhood was in foreign countries, where the individual shopkeepers still survive. And since we had no refrigerators (ice boxes only), shopping was at least an every other day occurrence, as was haggling with the vegetable shopkeeper.

It was on Intervale Street that I kissed my first girl. At five years old at Tootsie's birthday party, I took her behind the door and gave her a kiss on the cheek. Why is it we all remember our first kiss? Of course I learned later what a real kiss consisted of.

In 1939, my father felt flush enough to find a larger

apartment and to get closer to work. We moved several miles up Blue Hill Avenue to 67 Goodale Road in Mattapan. It was a two-bedroom apartment in a six-unit complex at the top of a very steep hill. While the location changed, we were still in the Jewish ghetto. All our friends were Jewish, and one heard a lot of Yiddish being spoken. (Sorry about being so specific about where we lived and dates. It all stems from my genealogic background.) The apartment was still cramped. We created a third bedroom out of what was supposed to be a dining room, which had doors with glass panels. Hardly conducive to privacy! It was in there that Ma and Pa slept, except when Pa was working; I slept in the same bed with my mother for at least a couple of years. (OK, you therapists: how did sleeping with my mother screw me up? After all, it was quite comfortable.)

Did I ever tell you that your grandmother spoke mainly Yiddish for many years, as did your grandfather? That was the language of the house. I could understand them but had to reply in English. They wanted me to be an American, speaking the American language. But I used to look at the Yiddish paper, *The Forward* (or *Forvitz*, as Pa pronounced it). It had photos on the back page with captions in both English and Yiddish—very helpful in learning the language. It was a socialist, liberal sheet that still exists, although printed in English. I even subscribed to it for a while in an effort to keep up with news about the Jewish community worldwide. But as the years went on and as I moved farther and farther from the ghetto, I lost the sense of community, that sense of knowing and caring about your neighbor.

I remember one time when we were visiting Boston, you remarked that Lou knew much about the history of Boston after he had taken you both on a tour of historic sites. I agreed that he knew history but that was not the Boston that I knew. I invited you both, but Tim declined (enough of Dad), to see my

Boston. I took you, Evelyn, to Intervale Street, but the house was gone, having been destroyed during one of the riots of the late sixties and seventies. The Jews had mostly moved out and it was now a black (African-American) ghetto.

I took you to Franklin Field and tried to describe the crowds that paraded along Blue Hill Avenue during the Jewish Holidays, with all the teens sitting on the stone wall that bordered the Park. We dropped by the Hecht House, and I described Haym Solomon AZA, which held its weekly Sunday meetings there. I tried to have you imagine the crush of people in front of the several synagogues on Woodrow Avenue. We even went to Boston Latin School and, surprisingly, the doors were open and we were free to wander the corridors.

At the end of the day, I was quite surprised at your comment, Evelyn, which has stuck with me for more than twenty years. You said that you envied me because I grew up in a COMMUNITY, not just an assemblage of homes, as the burbs are. You enabled me to see the strengths that came from that lower-middle-class, or upper-lower-class, setting. That idea of social interaction with your neighbors and friends has stuck with me all my life. I see a lot of it in you two.

There were two times that I strongly remember that sense of community. The first was on those hot Boston nights in a time of no air conditioning. The parents sat out on their stoops hoping for a small breeze. They talked and gossiped through the night while we, the kids, played in the street. We knew the neighbors and they knew and watched out for us. The second memory occurred during the war years. Joe and Lou were on bombers stationed in the South Pacific. We had a banner in our window with two stars on it. Virtually every home on the street had a banner in a window. And at the bottom of the hill, where Goodale Road intersected with Blue Hill Avenue, there was a large banner stretched across the street at the tops of two utilities poles. The banner showed the number of people in the armed forces of everyone living on that street.

What I remember most was the day when everyone gathered at the bottom of the street as the banner was taken down and replaced with one with a gold star. The gold star indicated someone had died in the war. The whole street met to mourn and cry. It just occurred to me that you two have not lived in a time of a popular war. Korea, Vietnam, Iraq have never engendered such whole-hearted support and pride.

I do not remember our family having that same experience, even though Joe died during the war. Perhaps it was because he died less than three weeks before the war ended. We did not even receive the telegram telling us that he was missing in action until after VJ Day, Victory over Japan Day, September 2, 1945. We got the news on September 7, after celebrating for several days that our family had survived the war intact.

The air force indicated that he had died on a mission while flying over Japan. The plane was apparently damaged on that mission. They told us that the crew probably was heading across the Korean peninsula in an attempt to make it to more friendly territory in China. Unable to maintain their altitude they crashed into a mountain in the southern part of Korea. They were the only Americans to die in Korea during the Second World War! There is even a monument on the site, erected by the Korean people. I visited there in 1988.

But Lou, who was apparently stationed on an island near Joe's island, heard about the crash on the same day as it occurred. Lou and his crew took their B-29 to the area (an unauthorized flight) to see if they could find Joe's plane. One time I asked Lou how he knew where to search. He indicated that the mission to Japan was only a cover story. The plane was headed for Korea to find out how far the Russians had progressed down the peninsula. We fought with the Russians, but President Truman did not trust them. And with good reason, as later years would show.

The war had been tough on those back home. Everything was poured into the war effort. I remember ration books. Everyone needed coupons to buy most foods. The coupons limited the home front consumption of foods in order that more would be available for the war fronts. Perhaps the only time you two have experienced anything like this was when you ran out of money during your days away at college.

And the cutback also included home building. Few new homes or apartments were built during the war years. In 1946 and 1947 millions of men and women were released from the service and headed home. Except, in many cases, there were neither homes nor apartments. In our case the owner of our apartment house had a son returning. They needed a place for him to stay. We were evicted from our apartment. I guess neighborliness extended only so far. The only way your grandfather could find a place for his family was to buy a home. He purchased a three-story apartment building and we moved less than two miles to 67 Astoria Street, still in the Mattapan neighborhood of Boston. I was twelve years old.

Perhaps this is a good time to stop and talk about the relationship that was most influential in my early years. While neighbors and friends talked about their, or the family's, illnesses, there were certain rules that were observed. Never talk about life-threatening diseases! Cancer was the "big C" and was only fully discussed after the hapless person had died. Illness, while the subject was alive, was more gossip than the subject of serious discussion. Anything serious took the discussion to an unwanted level.

And never, never, never talk about mental problems or mental diseases. Mental problems were not diseases, but rather something that was not quite a disease but also something that was not quite in the control of the person.

I remember my mother as being the one who took care of

the home. She shopped almost on a daily basis. She cooked wonderful meals on a gas stove which also had a kerosene-fed component. That part of the stove was used to heat the kitchen in the winter. The meals were kosher, thus meat and dairy were never mixed. As a result, my diet was much more varied than it has ever been since. Ma washed our clothes, using a washboard, by hand in the big kitchen sink. They were hung out on the lines spread across the back porch. In the wintertime they were frozen stiff and had to be warmed before they could be ironed on the drop-down ironing board hidden behind a panel in the kitchen. She cleaned the house, made the beds. She provided the warmth.

Yet, your grandmother was schizophrenic. I am not sure that most doctors even knew what to call it back then. As the years went on she became increasingly out of touch with reality. She spent much time in bed, and when awake she talked to herself, always mumbling, and talking to the people in the walls. They and others were trying to do harm to her family. She was our protector from all of these evil forces.

We were afraid to allow her to go out of the house by herself because there was no way of knowing what she would or could do. And except for Uncle Meyer, her brother, we rarely mixed with other members of the extended family. I was the one person in the family she trusted. As a result, I was responsible for her care. It was a daily struggle to make sure that she took her injection of insulin. I think that she believed that this was just another way that those voices were trying to harm her. So, in a strange way, for many of my teen years I took care of Ma while she took care of me. I felt the burden, and still do, of those years of responsibility.

The move to Astoria Street was not direct. We had to wait until one of the apartments in Pa's new home was vacated, which might take some time given the housing shortage. Pa began eviction proceedings against one of the tenants. In March of 1947 we put our furniture in storage and moved into one of the few apartments available, a beach cottage in Revere. This was an important event because it was the first time I was not under the protective chuppah of the Jewish ghetto. I came face to face with anti-Semitism.

It didn't make any sense to switch school systems, since we would be in Revere for only a few months (March to November, as it turned out). Each day I would commute two hours to the Solomon Lewenberg Junior High School in Mattapan and two hours back to Revere. It was quite a walk from the bus stop to our cottage. One day I was confronted by four boys about my age (twelve), white tee shirts, pants, Irish-looking. I heard names that I had only seen in print before (the *Forvitz*) or had heard on radio news reports. "Kike, Jew boy, what are you doing here?" they demanded. "Wanna fight?"

I was a pretty chubby kid at the time and had played at battles (cowboys and Indians) in the street with my friends but never anything real. I would like to say that I thought this through thoroughly, weighing the pros and cons, face them now or face them later. I heard someone say, "Yes." I realized it was me!

One of the boys stepped out and threw a punch at me. I hit him back and we rolled around on the ground for a while. I would like to say that I won, but that would not be true. In a few minutes I was on my back on the ground with him on his knees straddling me, throwing punches. "I quit," I yelled. He got up and the four of them left. I am sure that their stereotype of the Jew had been verified. It was not a Hollywood ending. I never told my family about this. I am not sure if it was because I lost, because I had been hurt, or because I had let Jews down. (What an ego! I had let the JEWS down.)

Despite this, beach living was not all that bad. The cottage was pretty basic. Beach homes were devoid of any amenities: no heat during the cold months and hot like a baker's brick oven in the summer. When the summer folks moved into their cottages, everything came alive. My friend Ernie, from Goodale Road, lived a few streets away, and we spent most of the day in the cold Atlantic ocean. Our natural olive skin became dark and darker. Our white eyes peered through dark brown lids. I was aware that the Irish were all around us, but they left us alone, and the Jews rarely mingled with them. I never had to fight again.

When the summer crowd left I could walk straight down the lonely beach without weaving in and out of beach blankets, chairs and umbrellas. The beach was cold and bleak, devoid of people. I loved it! There was comfort in the solitude. I was alone and did not mind it. In November we moved to the third floor of our new home on Astoria Street.

The years 1947 to 1948 were a pivotal period in my life. I am not sure if they were the most important years of my life but certainly a key period: a new home; new experiences (anti-Semitism); probably the only thing close to a long vacation that my family had together (the beach house); my Bar Mitzvah; new friends; Boston Latin School; and AZA.

I am not sure how I came to the decision, but I decided to leave the neighborhood school, Solomon Lewenberg Junior High School, and apply to Boston Latin School. Latin School was what we today would call a magnet school. It drew high-achieving students from all over the city. A student needed high marks (or, absent high marks, an entrance exam) to be accepted. Somehow I had grades good enough to allow me to be accepted.

Latin School is the oldest high school in the country (established 1635) and reeks with tradition: Latin declamations; not a principal but rather a "headmaster," who sat in a 150-year-old chair during the declamations. The dress code, which had recently dropped a requirement to wear jackets, still required that we wear ties. It was a unisex school with only male teachers, and a college prep curriculum. In one year my coursework consisted of English, Latin, French, ancient Greek, math and phys ed. It was definitely not a school geared to preparing its students for the job market. In 1952 I graduated in a class of 198 students, all of whom had been accepted by some college or university. About 125 had applied to Harvard, about 100 were accepted and about eighty attended. Almost seven percent of my Harvard entering class came from this single school!

The major impacts of Latin School upon me were two. First, a realization that learning didn't stop at graduation, it was a lifelong venture. Something I still believe and practice. Second, I met people who became my friends and who introduced me to Haym Salomon AZA. AZA, which still exists, was a junior version of B'nai B'rith. It was supposed to be a service organization but there was a lot of fun in that service. We had our weekly meetings, secret rituals, and yes, even a secret handshake. There were quite a number of AZA chapters around the city and we competed with them in sports. Our major activity was raising money for a scholarship which was given to someone in the community. It's funny to think that the scholarship which was only a few hundred dollars would mean much, until you realize that tuition at Harvard at that time was about $600 per term! Many of the members of AZA became lifelong friends, whose stories you can read in other chapters of this book.

AZA, like many events in this letter, deserves a chapter unto itself. Yet, if this letter is to be kept to reasonable length, AZA has to be kept to a few paragraphs. Studies in the field of psychology have indicated that peers are equally, if not more important than family in the formation of a person's personality. One key impact of my membership in AZA is that it led to a lifelong desire to be active in social groups of one kind or another, usually in some kind of official capacity. More about these later.

In June 1952 I graduated from Boston Latin School and in

September entered Harvard. At that time I still had the desire to become a medical doctor and thus majored in chemistry, thinking it would give me an advantage in any future applications to medical schools. By the time I reached calculus and physical chemistry, I realized that I did not have "it" for a medical profession. Unlike today's students, who may have several majors before graduating, I could not admit that I had made a mistake and stuck it out. I graduated about midway in my graduating class of about a thousand.

Harvard was not the rewarding experience that it might have been. With limited money and, at that time, little or no availability of education loans, I was forced to commute for the entire four years. There was little opportunity to experience the out-of-class learning that is so necessary in college. With tuition at $600 a term, it was still possible during the summer to make enough money to pay for a substantial portion of college costs, but not enough to pay for room and board. Pa, sixty-three years old when I entered Harvard, was still eking out a living as a baker. (With little retirement income, something he would do until he was in his eighties.) Until about the last year in college, commuting meant public transport. About 1955, Lou gave me his old DeSoto, and I finally could drive to Harvard. Each day I would drive the forty-five-minute to one-hour trip with three other commuters who helped pay for the gas (one AZA buddy and a woman who later married another AZA friend).

As an aside let me explain a little about the part-time jobs during my school years. I began working at thirteen years of age, when we moved to Astoria Street. During the weekends, and after returning home each day from Latin School, I worked at a small, local family-owned grocery store. When I say small, I mean small! The store was probably no more than 400 square feet. It had barrels of pickles and sauerkraut. Shelves ran all the way to the ceiling and I was adept at grabbing boxes off the top shelf with a long-handled "grabber" and dropping them easily into my arms. It had a small deli counter with real lox cut to order, lots of smoked fish, fresh bakery products. My job was to wait on customers and to deliver orders. The store had a push wagon and I would load the orders into the wagon, push the wagon for several blocks, and then carry the orders (two to four boxes, more during Passover) up two or three flights of stairs. About half the time I would receive a nickel tip. My weekly salary, as I remember it, for six days of work, was nine dollars.

After entering college, during the summer months at first, I worked as a "soda jerk" at a chain of ice cream restaurants, Brighams'. Then for a couple of summers I drove an ice cream truck up and down the streets of Everett, a Boston suburb. My experience at the grocery store became valuable because I was adept at having customers, who came out on their third-floor porches, and dropped the money for the ice cream into my waiting arms. I would then flick the ice cream (sandwich, popsicle, cone) up to the third floor. I also worked every day, for two hours each day, cleaning the dormitory rooms of grad students. During school holiday breaks I made more money by working for the university.

I came out of Harvard, in 1956, with a few new friends and acquaintances; a little bit of knowledge; a sharply honed skill at bridge, which I played every day at Dudley House, Harvard's commuter center; a taste for beer at Cronin's; many AZA buddies; and absolutely no idea about what I wanted to do with my life. I was convinced that I was not cut out for a life in a laboratory.

The country still had a draft, and every male was required to serve their country in the military for some period of time. The choice was a two-year commitment with no requirement to serve in the reserves after those two years, or six months with a reserve requirement that lasted several years. Having the possibility of being called up in the reserves hanging over my head for several years did not appeal to me. The "Cold War" seemed to have a habit of heating up every once in a while. I enlisted in the army and began my two-year hitch in September of 1956.

The one complicating factor was Ma's schizophrenia, which had grown progressively worse. In retrospect I probably could have obtained a "hardship" deferment, but it never occurred to me at the time. Then, in 1956, the thing that we feared most happened. She attacked a shopkeeper who she thought was trying to injure her and her family. We were under a court order to have her committed, and she spent the rest of her life in a mental institution near our home. I visited her often; the conditions there have to be experienced. No words can ever describe the conditions in that state hospital. The movie *The Snake Pit* comes close to a re-creation of the environment. But that movie only affects two senses, the eyes and ears. All five senses were attacked every time I entered that hospital. It was tough leaving her and home!

I arrived at Fort Dix, New Jersey, in September and began eight weeks of basic training. I entered the army at six feet two inches, and about 220 pounds. Eight weeks later I was still six-two, but had been trimmed down to less than 200 pounds. I was in the best physical shape that I would experience for a long time. But the most important aspect of army life was the other recruits. I realized that for most of my life I lived with and knew people who were pretty much like me: white, urban, democratic, education-oriented, from the Northeast. Now, in basic training, I met, lived with, and trained with people from all over the country. The group ranged from people who lived in small towns in Appalachia, never having been more than fifty miles from home, to well-educated, well-traveled people from the upper echelons of society. It was a great learning experience and tended to weld a disparate group into a single working group, whose only tie was the obligation to do service for the country. The experience led me to the belief that dropping the draft in the 1980s was a terrible decision. We no longer have the army as a force to produce a cohesive citizenship. Despite opinions to the contrary, the United States is not, nor ever was, a melting pot. It is more of a stewing pot, with large distinguishable pieces in one large pot, but hardly melted together. (If you do not believe me, ask yourself why every major urban city has a "Chinatown.") By doing away with the draft, the country lost the opportunity to produce a somewhat more unified nation.

After basic training the army noted that I had a degree in chemistry and sent me to Fort Monmouth to learn how to operate and repair field radios. It made no sense whatsoever. After a few weeks at Fort Monmouth I requested and received a transfer to the Army Chemical Corps. I was sent to the Army Chemical Center in Edgewood, Maryland, just outside Baltimore. There I spent almost two years working with poison gasses, phosgene and chloropicrin. But almost everyone on the post was white and college educated. I was back with people who were just like me.

The time at the chemical center was mostly one long party. With that many science majors, all of who had not learned any self discipline in college, the military discipline on the base was nonexistent. There were parties at the local tavern every weekend night. They were either "hump day" (one year in and one year to go) parties or "getting out" (done!) parties. We were AWOL most of the time. I also made extra money by operating the grill in the USO building. The best thing about this was that I had access to the refrigerator, which I kept filled with beer. Finally, there was a massive court martial on the base as the army tried to regain control. Fortunately, it occurred one month after I finished my service requirement and I had left the post.

I had hoped that the army would straighten me out and

provide some direction. But that was not the case. Several months before I was discharged I had a conversation with an AZA buddy (Arthur Cohen) who had attended the Harvard Business School. He convinced me to apply to the "B" School, which I did, and was the most surprised person when I was accepted. I remember the first day on campus. I went to the admissions office and told them that I had just completed two years in the army and had no money. They told me not to worry and I never did. I lived at the school, and this became the college experience that I had missed in the undergraduate college. For two years, except for some time at home on some weekends to visit Ma in the hospital, the school was my entire life.

My education, room and board were financed through loans, scholarships, and work opportunities. I ran the newsstand (candy, cigarettes, snacks, etc.) inside the dining building, which was open during dining hours. It was quite profitable and had a strange lasting effect. For years later I would run into alums who would say that they recognized me but could not quite place me. Of course the entire classes of 1958, 1959, and 1960 had seen me everyday at the stand!

The curriculum was rigorous. The case method of teaching required long nights and weekends of study. A great emphasis was placed on class participation, explaining and defending one's position. Presenting one's arguments in front of ninety classmates was, for me for a long time, a terrifying experience. But somehow, I made it through, again about midway in the pack, and graduated in 1960.

Tim and Evelyn, I am going to change this letter a bit. I have tried to give you a bit of history of our family and a bit of my early life. It has been mainly chronological. I want to now tell the rest of my story in terms of themes: Billie, work, groups, interests, regrets, and wisdom.

Billie: I fell in love with Billie almost from the moment I met her. How we met is one of the family stories that must be recorded. Billie Purchas (b. Vander Meulen) left the Midwest in 1965 for a new job (programming computers) in Manhattan and, as she would admit later, to meet a tall, Jewish man. She answered an ad for someone who was seeking a person to share an apartment. And so she met Mary Burns, who happened to be dating Ray Leiter, another AZA buddy, and who was sharing my apartment. In mid-February, Mary introduced me to Billie. I had been living the good New York life as a bachelor for almost five years. I think I was ready to settle down. Plus, Billie was the sexiest woman I had ever seen!

I helped Billie move into the apartment when her stuff arrived in Manhattan. Amidst that stuff was a cat, Orpheus. Unfortunately, Mary was allergic to cats. Billie had to get rid of Orpheus, so she asked me to take her cat into my apartment. I said it was OK, but if I took the cat, it would become mine.... Billie could not tell me how to care for Orpheus. (That alone should have given Billie some clues about my personality.) She reluctantly agreed.

Three months later, in June, Billie and I were sitting in my apartment and I asked Billie to marry me. At that moment Orpheus walked across the room. Billie looked at the cat, looked at me, and asked, "If I marry you do I get my cat back?" I said, "Sure," and she said, "Then, OK."

We were married in October, eight months after we met. Orpheus is long gone but forty-three years later Billie and I are still together.

Billie was not raised Jewish but she, on her own, decided to convert. I have been often asked if the cultural differences were a problem in the marriage. What I have learned is that the biggest strains in any marriage are not cultural, nor differences in backgrounds, nor life experiences. The biggest problem is that a marriage consists of a man and a woman (at least until recently).

The stuff that we bring into a marriage is more shaped by our gender than anything else. We somehow dealt with this and continue to successfully deal with it now. It was hard work but got a little easier over time.

About fifteen years ago, Billie was fighting breast cancer. She won. It was a wake-up call. She quit her position in the computer field and went back to grad school to get an MSW degree. For the past several years she has had a successful career as a psychotherapist. She is good at it; it is very rewarding on many levels.

Work: One of the first things to realize about my work experience is that none of the five companies for whom I worked still exist. They were all merged into other, larger companies. The second thing to realize is that I never had a career. I had a series of jobs with various companies. I never really thought about the long term. I approached each day as a new day with little thought of where each day was taking me.

Upon graduation, I was employed by M&T Chemicals, responsible for market research and market analysis . After four years there, I was tired of that and went to Freeport Sulphur, again running the market analysis department. After about eighteen months, I got a call from M&T Chemicals. They wanted me back and made me a nice offer. I went back and worked for them until 1970.

Again I was bored and wanted to try marketing products myself. I received an offer from the Permacel Division of Johnson & Johnson. I found that it was easier to advise marketers than to be one. I lasted at Permacel about two years. I left there in 1972 to do long-range planning for Anaconda. In 1976, the company was acquired by ARCO. I was asked to go to the corporate headquarters in Los Angeles to help Arco executives understand and integrate this nine-billion-dollar (sales) acquisition into their operations. After two years there I asked for and received a transfer in 1979 to ARCO Chemical Co. in Philadelphia.

I stayed at ARCO until retirement, in 1991. To a large extent this last job was my ideal job. I essentially functioned as an internal consultant. The only constant was that I was responsible for putting together the long-range plan each year. Other than that, each year represented new challenges, new studies and new projects. For the last eighteen months I worked in the public affairs department of ARCO. In this position, I worked closely with our office in Washington and functioned somewhat as a lobbyist. I even wrote and had a law passed giving ARCO a tax break on certain imported chemicals. I had a very good look at behind-the-scenes Washington. Frightening!

The latter part of 1991 was one of those momentous periods: I knew I was leaving ARCO; Lou died suddenly of a heart attack; and Tim was in an accident that almost resulted in complete paralysis. In the end we survived all of this. Proving again that this, too, shall pass!

I knew that I could not sit still for very long. For me, retirement was not something to be desired; it was more to be dreaded. (I could also use the money that more employment would bring.) I wanted nothing more to do with corporate life and wanted to be my own boss. In April 1992, I opened a party store under the PartyLand franchise in a Philadelphia suburb near my home. Two years later I took over a second party store in a large shopping center near King of Prussia. I realized soon that I had been tainted by the corporate mentality. Operating two stores would lead to three, then more. I sold the first store, doubled the size of the second and have operated that store for the past thirteen years. It has been rewarding in many ways.

Billie and I even went into business together. When we moved to East Windsor, New Jersey, in 1968, we wanted to enroll you, Evelyn and Tim, in a nursery school. The closest school was several miles away in Princeton. We enrolled you.

Each day Billie would drive you to the school. By the time she returned home it was almost time to make the return trip to pick you two up. We had moved into a newly constructed home in a new development amidst many new developments. Lots of families looking for childcare facilities.

We therefore rented a building, hired two teachers, purchased the equipment and started a Montessori School near our home, which from the start was at capacity, fifty students. When you two moved from that school to the first grade in public school, we sold the business. To my knowledge that school is still in operation.

Groups: One hallmark of my life after graduation is that I seem to enjoy being in and involved with social groups. My first job was in New York City, and I decided to become active in the Harvard Business School Club of New York. I was vice president for membership, which reached 2,000, the highest it has been before or since! I also ran programs for a couple of years and after that, published the HBS Club of N.Y. newsletter. I was a member of the board of directors for many years and received a number of awards from that organization. Every year the business school would hold an alumni conference for leaders of the various HBS clubs (about fifty) around the country. For several years I was asked to attend that conference and talk to the leaders about ways of building membership.

When I moved to L.A., in 1977, I joined the HBS Club of L.A. and was a major participant in putting together a large HBS conference in that city. Two years later, when I returned east, I joined the HBS Club of Philadelphia, only to find that the organization was moribund. I became president of that group, put together a board of directors and helped energize that organization to the point that it is still very active today.

The alumni organization at the business school in Boston was appreciative of my work, and I was elected to a three-year term on the HBS council. This is group of about fifty alumni who met regularly with the dean and others to represent the thousands of alumni. Being on that group was a significant honor.

When I returned to Philadelphia, I discovered the Jewish Genealogical Society and became involved in that group. I was elected VP of membership. In addition I gave many lectures to Jewish groups in the city about Jewish genealogy.

When I was in L.A. I wanted to improve my public speaking ability. I was instrumental in forming a chapter of Toastmasters International within ARCO. When I moved to Philly, I started another chapter there and became president of that group. I also helped establish other Toastmaster groups in other organizations.

Ten years ago, I became interested in Ikebana (the Japanese art of flower arranging). For four years I acted as treasurer of the Ikebana Society of Philadelphia. All this was after I had served as president of my local rotary club.

Interests: The list of organizations with which I have been involved pretty much defines my outside interests; for example, Jewish genealogy as expressed in developing my family tree. This culminated in my putting together the first Gorman family reunion in Boston just three years ago. Over 100 family members attended from several countries. It was a wonderful experience, and I learned more about my family, including the fact that a Gorman relative had been on Schindler's list! Very rewarding.

I never got over the folk music craze that was full blown in the fifties and sixties. It has been a continual interest. Billie and I still get together every few weeks with a group of friends (three guitarists, one bass player, and one banjo strummer) to sing for a few hours (shades of Lawrence Welk!). Very therapeutic!

During my years in Boston, Helen always had a subscription

to some theater group. On occasion, something would prevent her from attending the performance so she would give me her ticket. I fell in love with the theater instantly. During the years in New York I attended the theater as much as I could afford. Since Billie and I have been married, we have each year had at least one, two, three or four theater and orchestra subscriptions. Very stimulating!

My major interest in recent years has been Ikebana. The group to which I belong consists of 150 women and three men. This is peculiar to the West, because in Japan men are much more involved in this art form. The founder, in 1850, of the school in which I study, the Ohara school, was a man, as were the founders of many of the other major schools. I have been studying in this school for ten years, which makes me pretty much of a novice. For about eight months of the year I attend weekly classes. Once a month the U.S. grandmaster comes to Philadelphia to teach a day-long class. I usually attend these.

In March of each year, Philadelphia is the location of the oldest and largest flower show in the country. In 2006 and 2007 I was asked to provide arrangements at the Ikebana booth at the show. I loved it!

While Ikebana is an interest, cooking is somewhat of a passion. I think that this is a legacy from my father. Not only was he a great baker, he was also a terrific cook. When I moved into New York, I would prepare gourmet meals for my friends out of a very tiny kitchen. Later, Billie and I would often have twenty or more people for brunch, dinner or just an English tea. We used to have dinners in which someone was murdered (before the meal) and the meal participants had to find the murderer. Great fun!

Regrets: As I indicated, learning is a lifelong experience. I have tried to live this idea and have rarely not been involved in some class or learning experience. When I settled in New York after graduating from the "B" School, I realized that I probably would not do much reading, on my own, in the business field. I knew that if I were in an academic setting I would keep up. So I enrolled at NYU Business School (evening division). I had no desire for a PhD but if I changed my mind later any courses taken to that point would not count for the program. Enrolling in the PhD program was pretty easy.

In 1962 I began, and as the years passed I got closer and closer to finishing the program. I passed the language requirement, passed all the written exams and in 1968 passed the three-hour oral exam, defending three fields: economics, management, and marketing. All that was left was the thesis.

But at this point my ADD set in (that's as good an excuse as any) and I never finished. My thesis proposal was to examine the field of childcare as an opportunity for a national business. Most nursery schools and childcare facilities at that time were "mom and pop" operations. It seemed to me that social and other forces would greatly increase the need for more rigorous childcare facilities, i.e. a great business opportunity. Years later I was proved right as several national companies were formed that offered franchises in the field of childcare.

My major regret is that I never completed the thesis and today I am merely an AbD (All but the Dissertation)!

Wisdom: Writing this letter has caused me to ask a couple of related questions: What are my core beliefs? What wisdom have I gleaned after almost seventy-five years?

I do not know how to write this without having it sound like a lot of platitudes. But here goes.

One of my core beliefs, perhaps influenced by my study of "the invisible hand" of economics, is that of personal responsibility. We are responsible for the good that comes out of our actions and must bear the consequences of the bad. That is true not only at the personal level but also on the national level.

A second core belief is that nothing is set in stone. Every day is a new opportunity for change. I truly believe that the greatest gift that we receive is a new day...each day full of possibility and fun. It could be something as simple as taking some flowers and putting them together in an arrangement that pleases the senses. Or the change could be as complex as changing one's life direction. Each day is a clean slate.

My entire wisdom after seventy-five years consists of a couple of simple thoughts. The first is, like my kidney stones, this too shall pass. Everything which seemed enormously important fades into obscurity over time. It takes time to put the events of our lives into perspective. Whatever you do, have some fun in the process.

And the second thought is contained in one of my favorite poems. The poem was written about thirty-five years ago by Theodor Geisel (Dr. Seuss) and was delivered at a college commencement. Here is "My Uncle Terwilliiger on the Art of Eating Popovers."

My Uncle ordered popovers
from the restaurant's bill of fare.
And when they were served,
he regarded them with a penetrating stare....
Then he spoke great words of wisdom
As he sat there on his chair:
"To eat these things," said my uncle
"you must exercise great care.
You may swallow down what's solid....
But you must spit out the air!"

And as you partake of the world's bill of fare,
That's good advice to follow.
Do a lot of spitting out the hot air,
And be careful what you swallow.

Tim and Evelyn, I keep wanting to go back and add to this letter. Any of these paragraphs could be expanded into separate chapters. I have left out so many stories. I have not at all written about how proud I am of you two. Tim, I am proud of your bronze medal win in 1993 and the gold medal win at the 1997 rugby Maccabi games in Israel. Evelyn, you have proudly represented the U.S. in Dragon Boat racing in international events in China, Germany and Australia. Each of you has had fascinating work and life experiences. I am just proud of who you both are. Perhaps this letter will encourage each of you to write your stories.

I will be interested in your reaction to this letter.

Lots of Love,
Dad

Epilogue to the Book

I HAVE HAD THE SINGULAR privilege of editing these stories of my fellow Alephs of Haym Salomon. For me this effort has been a labor of love—a wistful return to my boyhood friends from the Hecht House and The Wall at Franklin Field in Boston.

It was not easy for most of us to find it within ourselves to tell the stories of our lives. We are more or less private guys, politically liberal for the most part but emotionally conservative, and so the stories here told emerged only with mutual prodding and support. Often the carrot was that these, the stories of our lives, as we interpret our lives, merit passing on to our children and our children's children, a kind of reliving of the Passover duty to tell our children of the escape from bondage in Egypt.

As we have read through these lives, these stories, we have noted first, that most of the Alephs came from two-parent homes and they were very secure within the families of their childhood, even when those families were what some might nowadays view as "dysfunctional": distant fathers, overly protective mothers, with parental conflicts and financial troubles at home. But the matriarchies of our Dorchester and Roxbury days were legendary, and they provided us with the stability and security which were the essential bases of our lives, without which nil that followed would have been possible. We Alephs of Haym Salomon AZA emerged from these tough but relatively stable, mostly working-class, Dorchester and Roxbury Jewish family backgrounds as strong personalities, to become in time the rocks, really, of our own nuclear families. We were, and are still, at seventy-four and beyond, looked to, even relied upon by our wives and our children. We once-and-always Alephs took and continue to take, albeit now in modified form, our practical and emotional/psychological responsibilities very seriously.

Secondly, we were well educated—at Boston Latin, Roxbury Memorial and Boston English public high schools, where we excelled, and at Harvard, Yale, Tufts and elsewhere, where we also thrived—and we were professionally successful. Of the ten whose lives here have come before you, three were lawyers (two in private practice, one in government); four spent their professional lives in leadership positions in business or finance, often via a technical graduate or undergraduate education in engineering, finance, or chemistry; one was an academic physician-scientist; one a journalist; and one a writer/poet. We continue for the most part to be active in our trades or in related activities. Thus out of similar environmental conditions came our interestingly diverse group, which diversity is an important part of our stories and our appeal.

We were, as a group, special in some ways, unremarkable in others; but our affection for one another and support of one another was and remains nothing short of extraordinary, amazing really. It is a blessing of considerable proportions for each of us to have one another's good will and continued love.

Arthur Bloom

A Remembrance of

Irving Kenneth Zola

ONE DAY IN 1950, when Irving Zola was fifteen years old, he began to feel pain in his legs that would not go away. The pain soon became agony, as he experienced a feeling of ceaseless and utterly excruciating muscle cramps everywhere across his body. He had contracted polio, a disease now almost extinct, thanks to the development of vaccines not long afterward (the first of them released to the public by Dr. Jonas Salk only five years after Irving fell ill). But back then, the grim threat of polio hung over us all, especially young people, looming up anew every summer. The disease ravaged Irving Zola's legs and much of the rest of his body. He would wear leg braces for the rest of his life and walk with canes or crutches.

When he emerged from rehabilitation, he began to face his future, at first with desperation and rage. For a very brief time, he drank heavily but then he rapidly began to show the determination that would transform the rest of his life. Irving used to say that if he hadn't been stricken with polio, he would have become a businessman of some kind, and his intelligence and skill with numbers would have likely brought him considerable prosperity. (Among other financial skills, Irving was always good at poker and, before polio changed his life, he had been very successful in open-air poker games played way out in the grass at the local hangout of Franklin Field. Some of them took place during the High Holidays, while the elders were off praying in the synagogues. They were high-stakes games for working-class kids, where a whole week's salary could be lost, and Irving told a friend that he thought he had made enough in those games—and saved the money—to pay for a first year of college.)

Irving returned to high school with a developing sense of purpose, and scholarships would then carry him through Harvard all the way to a PhD in the Department of Social Relations. Even an auto accident while he was an undergraduate that left him seriously injured and subject to another long period of recovery did not diminish his will or his determination to live a positive life and not be delimited by the damage done to his body. Irving had immense sympathy for others as well as a sense of humor that could lead him to share jokes with everyone and sometimes, to roll on the floor with his close friends, all overcome with riffs of humorous exchange. He became an internationally known specialist in disability studies, published many articles and books, and was especially respected for his very personal memoir of his disability, *Missing Pieces,* published in 1982. He traveled the country and abroad as an advocate for the disabled and, among numerous other contributions to the general welfare, worked with Senator Ted Kennedy on the landmark Americans with Disabilities Act (the ADA) of 1990. On the personal level, he lived a rich and vigorous life that included two marriages: the first as a young man to Lee Cohen, during which they adopted two beloved children, Warren and Amanda Beth, and then a late, very happy marriage to the women's-health activist Judy Norsigian and the birth of his much-adored daughter Kyra. On December 1, 1994, when he was only fifty-nine, the damaged body he had mastered and compelled into his service through so many physically difficult years gave out suddenly and he died of a heart attack.

The word "hero" has come to be carelessly used in recent times, often applied to victims or casualties of war who, no matter how terrible and unjust their sufferings or deaths, are not heroes in the strict sense of the term. In military usage, for which medals are awarded, a hero is one who risks his or her life in order to save others or confronts the enemy with extreme bravery and thus lessens danger for his or her comrades. In almost the pure military sense of the term, Irving Zola was a hero. The enemy he faced was a malignant microbe and its effect, which could have plunged him into a life of lingering despair. Instead he bravely confronted that enemy, and the harshness of chance that can suddenly overturn a life. He had no comforting (for some) belief in a deity but refused to be diminished by his ferocious enemy, and harnessed the energy and creativity born from that refusal for his own and the world's good.

At the memorial service held for him at Brandeis University, where he spent many years as a professor, hundreds of friends, students, and admirers turned out to shower his memory with a flood of loving words and to do him heartfelt honor.

Hank Heifetz

APPENDICES

APPENDIX 1

Flyer announcing the Ninth Annual Scholarship Fund Ball of Haym Salomon AZA, to be held on April 21, 1953, at the Totem Pole ballroom in Newton, Massachusetts, at $2.40 per couple, with music provided by Johnny Long and the Orchestra. The flyers were widely distributed throughout the Greater Boston area. *(Original flyer courtesy of George Wolkon)*

APPENDIX 2

The Frank V. Thompson Junior High School marching band, 1950. *Front row, left to right:* Martin Hunt, Philip Shaeffer, Arthur Bloom, Marvin Lurie, Seymour Saslow, Irwin Kabler, and Neal [last name unknown]. *Back row, left to right:* unknown, unknown, Albert Perlmutter, Gordon Mirkin, unknown, unknown. Arthur Bloom and Irwin Kabler were members of Haym Salomon AZA (others may have belonged to different chapters of AZA). *(Photo courtesy of Irwin Kabler)*

APPENDIX 3

Members of the Haym Salomon AZA Chapter, at the 1953 Annual Scholarship Fund Ball, held at the Totem Pole Ballroom, Norembega Park, Newton, Massachusetts. The members at that time were: Arnold Abelow, Arnold Aronson, Leonard Baker, Jerry Bell, Arthur Bloom, Louis Bortnick, Joseph Burman, Eliot Burtman, Arthur Cohen, Norm Cohen, Jerry Davidow, Morris Dratch, Lou Fingerman, Sam Fish, Michael Garber, Norm Gordon, Jim Haine, Henry Heifetz, Richard Israel, Bob Jaspan, Irwin Kabler, Marv Kagan, Sumner Katz, Sheldon Kessler, Raymond Leiter, Allen Locke, Martin Mintz, Karl Norris, Don Orenbuch, Herb Rodman, Paul Rosenthal, Jerry Sadow, Arnold Saitow, Richard Savrann, Saul Shapiro, George Shore, Bob Shwartz, Jerry Silver, Charles Smith, Bernard Weisbladt, George Wolkon, Jordan Zisk, and Irving Zola. *(Photo courtesy of Irwin Kabler)*

APPENDIX 4

Former members of Haym Salomon AZA, at Harvard Hillel, June 4, 2006, on the occasion of the fiftieth reunion of the Harvard Class of 1956. *Front row, left to right:* Sheldon Kaufman, Arnold Aronson, Sam Fish, Jerry Sadow, Karl Norris, Ray Leiter, Arnie Abelow, Arthur Bloom, Sumner Katz; *Back row, left to right:* Paul Rosenthal, Herb Rodman, Bob Jaspan, Stephen Greyser, Norman Gordon, Don Orenbuch, Arnie Saitow, Jerry Davidow, Morris Dratch, Richard Savrann, Martin Mintz. *(Photo courtesy of Martin Mintz.)*